Ultimate Rest

The Essence of the Beautiful Gospel

David W. Hewitt

Foreword by Rod Williams

Wellsprings Community

FIRST EDITION 2024
Wellsprings Community
ISBN 978-1-7392680-2-2
Wellsprings Community, 71 Whitehill Street
Newcraighall, Edinburgh EH21 8QZ

Wellsprings Community is a registered Scottish charity SC040639

ACKNOWLEDGEMENTS

Front cover design is based on a beautiful painting by Audrey Dutton, used with permission. Audrey lives with her husband John and three boys on a farm in Nebraska.

She is a grace-orientated bible teacher and an artist, (see www.eatmedrinkmepodcast.net).

Thone Hupa and Christopher Hewitt were then responsible for finalising the cover design.

The rear cover includes an image of The Flowering Tree stained-glass window by Roger Wagner, located in Iffley Church, Oxford. The photo was taken by Simon Hodge and is included in publications with the permission of Roger Wagner (see rogerwagner.co.uk).

Grateful thanks are given to Rachel Hewitt and Marjory Morrow for contributing sections for the Appendix, to Heather Wright for her careful editing and to Ilir Mitrushi for assistance with formatting.

This book is dedicated to my
parents, Ken and Joy Hewitt,
who gave me a very happy
childhood and showed me
genuine love.

ENDORSEMENTS

I just finished reading Ultimate Rest and, no exaggeration, I could feel a tangible sweet fragrant breeze of the Holy Spirit blowing over me as I read! This doesn't surprise me at all because David and Maggie, and their family and the Wellsprings community they help steward, truly embody the beautiful Gospel of Jesus in an authentic way.

This book is an obvious natural outflow of their life. David has been a leading champion of an integrated prayerful & restful Trinitarian spirituality for years. I was encouraged at the many sources he ties together here, as well as the practical wisdom and advice this book details for a real life of Gospel rest. If you don't understand what the big deal is about 'rest,' please read this book! And, if you do, please use this book as a rich resource to spread the word!

Matt Spinks
Director, The Fire House Projects Co. Fort Wayne, author of *High on God*

Plagued by the shadows of anxious inner turmoil we cannot even diagnose, each of us longs for the green pastures of a distant, yet utterly familiar land that is our true home. The profound, perhaps infinite desire for authentic inner peace feels unrequited the more we grasp for it. We cannot generate rest. The panacea of leisure time or recreation, the momentary diversions of vapid entertainment or chronic 'doom-scrolling' (much less vain religious efforts to appease our restless sense of moral obligation to earn absolution) often do nothing but add to this nihilistic frustration.

Surely there are coping mechanisms that are more therapeutic than toxic … but how might we find deep repose that amounts to more than treading water? David Hewitt, with profound simplicity, explores how our innermost longing is not for mere stasis but an ek-stasis: we have already been carried home, even carried out of ourselves … Home has come to us. And this abode is in the very centre of the eternal, other-giving love of the Triune God. A gracious, unconditional love for which we have been created, are currently sustained and have indeed been restored in the Person of Christ.

Indeed, true rest is more than a static disposition, but an eternal Person who has already swept our humanity into His divine life. David's insightful volume speaks truth against our psychological clutter. He declares the only good news that can ultimately allay the subterranean tensions that drive our reactive minds and hearts: that far beneath our worst fears and crippling unease lies a much deeper abyss of pure acceptance. A bottomless divine rest that has already found us by sheer grace!

This book covers a ton of ground in a very accessible way. Really nice work.

John Crowder,
Founder of the New Mystics, Portland, author of seven books including *Mystical Union, Cosmos Reborn* & *Chosen for Paradise*.

It is said that you understand a subject when you can explain its complexities in a way that anyone can understand. In this book, David draws from personal experience, biblical insights and theological giants to expertly draw back the veil on often misunderstood passages of scripture, revealing the mystical heart of Christianity. There is so much here to enrich your spiritual life and liberate your soul in the experiential freedom that is given to us in the gospel. I highly recommend it to anyone who wants to understand what the Christian faith is all about or to go deeper in knowing Divine Rest.

Paul Golf
Senior Lecturer in Translation Studies, Bristol University UK, founder of Champions of Hope, developer of *Introducing the Trinitarian Faith.*

I love this book! In recent years, in my further discovery of union, I've been fascinated by the story of Jesus taking a nap on a boat in a storm. You know it—Jesus, awakened by fearful disciples, calms the storm. For years, I concluded that calming the storm was the destination, the focal point of this story. I constructed my faith on the faulty certainty that God calmed storms, instead of the sure foundation that God rests regardless of storms.

David Hewitt writes, 'True rest comes from knowing & flowing from a heart united with His.' In the noisy world of electronic distractions, hectic schedules, and our religious obsession with separation, he invites us to discover union and a *rest* that can't be compromised by storms.

David writes, 'The Biblical revelation of the incarnate Son of God is that we were formed to live in harmony with the Godhead–Father, Son, and Holy Spirit...we were designed for this state of rest.' What if, 'Jesus is the place of rest we were made for—to live in him, hidden in Christ in God.' And what if Jesus' nap was the fruit of union and, as David writes, 'This is the beautiful, good news of the Gospel?'

Ultimate Rest is an invitation to metanoia, to *theosis*, to sharing in the divine life. There is grace available in the pages of this book—grace to experience abundant life, community, inner freedom, and rest.

Jason Clark
Author of *Leaving and Finding Jesus, God Is (Not) In Control* & *Prone to Love,* Co-host of Rethinking God with Tacos podcast.

Imagine being with the disciples on the boat with Jesus. He's napping in the hull. You are frantically bailing water and freaking out at the size of the storm. We all know the rest of the story, but what if the invitation from Jesus was to come and rest with Him?

What if following Jesus looks like sleeping in a storm? David Hewitt provides a timely and refreshing reminder that 'Rest is directly linked to the grace of God'. Ultimate Rest is a Heavenly call back to the garden life where Peace is a Person, and you are vitally in union with Him. And yes, you may read this book on the Sabbath!

Derek Turner
Pastor at RiverCharlotte.com, Author of *Make Room - 21 Days with Jesus.* Co-host of Rethinking God with Tacos podcast.

Rest is not only a refrain from activity or work, but a posture shaped by the reality of Christ and his gospel. Instead of giving us another "how-to-unstress-your-life" handbook, David leads us to the place and the Person where all rest originates. He then carefully uncovers how the traditions of scripture and the Saints of old help us remain grounded in that place.

Reading David's book is like being taken on a pastoral walk along the Scottish coast! David has an ability to weave the reality of Christ into our lives, or rather, to show how we are woven into his. As you read, you will realize that rest is not something far off or hard to attain, but something you are *already* enveloped by, something you can dare to fall into.

Tobias Siegenthaler
PhD, School of Divinity, University of St Andrews, Scotland

Contents

FOREWORD

by Rod Williams

I agree with some of our friends who have nicknamed David Hewitt 'the kindest man in Scotland' and acknowledge that among His many roles that include architect, theologian, artist and sailor, he is also one who truly gives himself to lead others beside the still waters as pastor. His creative and kind heart comes through in Ultimate Rest.

Here we revisit our good and noble origin in the blessed Trinity and the promises of Jesus to rest in Him. We see where the theological thinking we inherited, and our bad choices, have affected peace in our practical lives. We learn to better operate from our inner man at rest and allow Holy Spirit to nurture peace and health.

This is not a "do more" and "try harder" kind of book but an invitation to increase our awareness of and value for rest, while allowing the kindness of God to change our minds.

For whoever enters God's rest also rests from his own work, just as God did from His. Let us, therefore, make every effort to enter that rest...
—Hebrews 4:10-11

In this age of the busy and bombarded mind, we may have more information and less understanding than any generation, as awareness of our inner life is swept away by a torrent of algorithmic conditioning and monetized outrage. We need quiet. We need rest.

We need sabbath. 'All of humanity's problems stem from man's inability to sit quietly in a room alone.'
(Blaise Pascal, Pensées)

We often lose touch with contemplative silence, where distractions lose their power and we hear Christ–who is the centre of all things and rest personified–call us back to the peace and significance of our original design.

We become what we behold, and part of the value of reading this book is taking time to slow down and focus, to allow our hearts to be set upon the beauty of Christ in us, the hope of glory, who is Himself our rest. Ultimate Rest refreshes our vision of fellowship with the mystery and helps return to the promise of Jesus:

Come to Me, all you who are weary and burdened, and I will give you rest. Take My yoke upon you and learn from Me; for I am gentle and humble in heart, and you will find rest for your souls.
—Matthew 11:28-29

Rod Williams
Author and speaker, Senior Coordinator and Professor at Cana Seminary and Professor at School of Kingdom, degree in Theology from Pacific Coast College.

INTRODUCTION

This book came about as I contemplated the amazing implications of the Gospel when viewed though a lens of the Trinity of Love. The title *Ultimate Rest* just dropped into my mind.

Having been aware of God's reality since my childhood–a sense of genuine encounter that has never gone away even during difficult times–I had to endure a number of years in which the emphasis in biblical teaching seemed to form a burden that made one feel slightly unsafe with regard to the holiness of God, obedience to church hierarchy and prospects for the 'end times'. When our relationship with God is made to look precarious, we can be thrown back on ourselves, and even though we might not say it openly, we subtly adopt a striving or forced religiosity.

I then began to read more widely and discovered that there were perspectives on the 'finished work of the Cross' that go back to the early Church Fathers. The Gospel message has been distorted at various times in history as one emphasis or another has been brought to bear, particularly in the last two centuries. When I delved deeper into teaching on the Trinity and the vicarious work of the Son of God, it was as if a weight lifted off my shoulders. Ever since, I have found that an understanding of the unrelenting, outrageous grace and goodness of God rings true in the core of my being. The Father *is* like the portrait Jesus gives us in Luke 15–the shepherd who goes after the lost sheep until he finds it, the woman who diligently recovers the lost coin and the father who, with lavish kindness, restores the undeserving son into the family home–and Jesus and the Father are one! As a little girl apparently once remarked, 'Jesus is the best picture the Father ever had took.' And as his death and resurrection approached, Jesus confirmed for us, *'In that day you will know that I am in my Father, and you are in me and I am in you'* (John 14:20), surely the fulcrum point of John's gospel. Now through the indwelling of the Holy Spirit we get to live in union with the Lord, day and night, living from his Life that flows through our beings. What a Gospel!

When we understand the breadth of the spiritual rest that God intended us to inhabit, physical *homeostasis* can easily follow. My daughter Rachel Hewitt has contributed an excellent chapter on this called Wild Wellness!–unrestrained wholeness as intended by our Creator–and our friend Marjory Morrow has produced a delightful meditation to help us bathe in the kindness of God. My thanks to them and the other members of Wellsprings Community who have encouraged me along the way–in particular to Heather Wright for her patient and careful editing of my manuscript–and to friends around the world who have spurred me on in sharing this message.

Enjoy the read, listen to the echo in your heart and sink back into God's Ultimate Rest!

David Hewitt, Edinburgh 2024.

ONE | We are made for rest!

Out of a dreamy miasma we are awakened with a start by our alarm! BZZZ, BZZZ, BZZZ! Morning! Daily checklists flood through the mind: kids to get up, breakfast to make, things that Must Not Be Forgotten for school, for mother, for the boss, for the deadline coming up today. Then out into the crush of the traffic, or the bus queue, clutching all we need for the day. Checking emails and social media, we are deluged by a stream of demands, desires, some delights, some disappointments ... our day is already being borne along by a plethora of things pulling us in many directions. And so it often continues until then, after the midday peak, we descend into the rush of afternoon and evening needs. School run, washing to hang out, shopping to pick up, phone calls to make, visit to the gym to fit in–the emotional drain of children squabbling, or office politics or family fall-outs–only to crawl onto the sofa and switch on the box to try and unwind, streaming a movie or catching up on news. And then the desire for intimacy! Sleep overcomes us as we set the alarm on our phone for the next day ... and longing for the holiday that is still months away ... only to repeat the cycle tomorrow.

This scenario may not precisely describe where your life is now, but for many people in the Western world, daily life is full of pressure. Pressure creates stress. Stress has detrimental effects on our bodies, our families, our relationships, our sense of identity. Deep down we know that this is not what we were designed for! Of course, things must be done, responsibilities met, children raised, bills paid. But at times it can feel as if the threads that weave the fabric of our lives can stifle the very enjoyment of living or, at best, force it to the fringes of our existence.

While it can't be proven in a laboratory, the spiritual side of our being cries out for attention. So we search and search for ways to satisfy this, some good and some maybe not so good. The growth of the wellness industry is testimony to this: some advice has been of genuine help to people (see a later chapter), while some is exploited by commercial interests keen to profit from the latest craze.

It has become commonplace in contemporary culture to disregard or dismiss the Bible as being anachronistic, bigoted or in some way irrelevant to our day–but to do so is to miss the wonder it contains regarding *us*. We should certainly be aware of the genre that a particular passage is written in and avoid unnecessarily literal or narrow interpretation. Yet as we open the pages of the Bible–the collection of ancient writings we know as the Scriptures– we can acknowledge that they were compiled and attested by the Church Fathers as being the reliable, God-breathed account of our place and meaning in this vast universe. We see there a significance in the pattern of creation. Most would now see the creation account in Genesis as parabolic, a story that presents Truth, while not necessarily being literal (the real meaning of myth). The existence of other creation stories in ancient cultures also clearly points to something deep in the human psyche about our origins that connects with our spirituality, as people try to describe something that scientific explanations cannot sufficiently explain.[1]

---

[1] For instance, the Mesopotamian *Enūma Eliš* contains numerous parallels with passages of the Old Testament. However, Genesis is monotheistic, it makes no attempt to suggest God's origin and there is no fighting to achieve the reduction of chaos as in the Mesopotamian versions. There are many so-called cosmogonical

What were the Divine purposes in creating mankind? The Biblical revelation of the incarnate Son of God is that we were formed to live in harmony with the Godhead–Father, Son and Holy Spirit–who from before time began lived in 'sweet community': a relationship of delight and other-centred love. Love can only exist in plurality (or it would be the narcissistic self-love of a monotheistic dictator) and the wonder of the Biblical narrative is that at the centre of the universe there exists, and has always existed, a God who by very nature is both One and Three. The Genesis account describes God as *them*, clearly indicating the triune nature of the divine. Yet, as Ephesians 1:4 makes clear, this was always intended to be shared: *'Even before he made the world, God loved us and chose us in Christ to be holy and without fault in his eyes.'* (NLT). Holiness, as Baxter Kruger points out, should be seen as a relational, rather than moral, state; the persons of the Trinity are set apart for one another, and we have similarly been set apart for God!

> *He associated us in Christ before the fall of the world. Jesus is God's mind made up about us....* (Eph 1:4 MIR)

The Trinitarian understanding, rooted in the Scriptures but unpacked for us in the early centuries by the Church Fathers, was that the Godhead–of one essence yet distinct in three persons–decided to widen this circle of love to include mankind and all of creation. Far from being the work of a distant or detached creator, we learn that everything was formed in and through Christ and is continually held together by his word of power (Col 1:16-17). So, the Greek idea of mankind needing to ascend a 'stairway' to reach God owes more to

---

myths, that is, they describe the ordering of the cosmos from a state of chaos. Yet, in Genesis God speaks with authority and the universe is created *ex nihilo* (out of nothing).

Plato and his friends than the teaching of the New Testament. Unfortunately, this idea has permeated the church[2] and is still common in evangelical or charismatic circles to this day. So Christian faith has assumed a reputation for *striving*, for the need for our effort after salvation to become sanctified and 'fit for heaven'. So many hymns and carols have echoed this notion, that we might attain a holy state through 'repentance' and right living.

Of course, this is not to say that *all* these things are wrong. God is Light from Light and absolutely pure in goodness and truth, and intends us to live this way too. 'Living our best life' is living in harmony with heaven. But if we think that this can be obtained by some human effort, or worse, some D.I.Y. religious practices, we've missed the whole wonder of the glorious Gospel. No, the fact is that what we were unable to do–could never do in a thousand years of trying–God did himself by entering our darkness and redeeming us 'from the inside'. With astounding humility and unrelenting love, he took on sinful flesh, was born of a young peasant girl and as the Last Adam lived our life in complete faithfulness, holiness and obedience. We had no part in this: *'But God showed his great love for us by sending Christ to die for us while we were still sinners.'* (Rom 5:8) As we read on in Colossians, we see that *'...through him God reconciled everything to himself. He made peace with everything in heaven and on earth by means of Christ's blood on the cross.'* (Col 1:20)

So, there was a return to something called **peace**; this peace is much more than a cessation of hostilities, or just quiet, pastel-shaded surroundings. Biblical peace implies a holistic state in which the

---

[2] St Augustine (Augustine of Hippo 354 – 430 AD) helped formulate the doctrine of original sin and is often cited as contributing to this view.

person is restored, healed and brought into harmony with God's order. The Hebrew *shalom* implies completeness, soundness, wellbeing, complete reconciliation–something inside as well as out–and the Greek *eirene* was a term which described a dovetailed joint in carpentry–the strongest possible connection–and also medically described the healing of a broken bone. We understand from surgeons that this mend becomes *even stronger* than the original.

After each stage of formation in Genesis, we hear that God says, 'It is good'. In fact 'The Jesus Children's Storybook Bible' has a beautiful paraphrase of this account:

> In the beginning there was nothing. Nothing to hear. Nothing to feel. Nothing to see. Only emptiness. And darkness. And ... nothing but nothing. But God was there. And God had a wonderful Plan.
>
> "I'll take this emptiness," God said, "and I'll fill it up! Out of the darkness, I'm going to make light! And out of the nothing, I'm going to make ... EVERYTHING!"
> Like a mommy bird flutters her wings over her eggs to help her babies hatch, God hovered over the deep, silent darkness. He was making life happen.
> God spoke. That's all. And whatever he said, it happened.
> God said, "Hello light!" and light shone in the darkness. God called the light, "Day" and the darkness, "Night." "You're good," God said. And they were.
>
> Then God said, "Hello land!" And there–splashing up through the oceans–came cliffs, mountains, sandy beaches. "You're good," God said. And they were.

"Hello trees!" God said. "Hello grass and flowers!" And Everything Everywhere burst into life. He made buds bud; shoots shoot; flowers flower. "You're good," God said. And they were.

"Hello stars!" God said. "Hello sun! Hello moon!" And whizzing into the darkness came fiery globes, spinning around and around–whirling orange and purple and golden planets. "You're good," God said. And they were.

"Hello birds!" God said. And with a fluttering and flapping and chirping and singing, birds filled the skies. "Hello fish!" God said and with a darting and dashing and wriggling and splashing, fish filled the seas! "You're good," God said. And they were.

Then God said, "Hello animals!" And everyone came out to play. The earth was filled with noisy noises–growling and gobbling and snapping and snorting and happy skerfuffling. "You're good," God said. And they were. God saw all that he'd made and he loved them. And they were lovely because he loved them.

But God saved the best for last. From the beginning, God had a shining dream in his heart. He would make people to share his forever happiness. They would be his children, and the world would be their perfect home. So God breathed life into Adam and Eve. When they first opened their eyes, the first thing they ever saw was God's face. And when God saw them he was like a new dad. "You look like me," he said. "You're the most beautiful thing I've ever made!" God loved them with all

> of his heart and they were lovely because he loved them. And Adam and Eve joined in the song of the stars and the streams and the wind in the trees, the wonderful song of love to the one who made them. Their hearts were filled with happiness. And nothing ever made them sad or lonely or sick or afraid. God looked at everything he'd made. "Perfect!" he said. And it was.

There is something in the essential quality that God affirms in the cosmos he has created: it is beautifully aligned to his intention for life. We know the story well: when Adam (literally 'man-made-of-soil') is formed, God's description is not just 'good', but '*very* good': perfect. Mankind is the ultimate act in creation in which the Godhead forms someone personal in their image.

After making man and providing for his well-being (Day Six in the Creation account) we read that God *rested* from his work, Genesis 2:2–he *shabath;* ceased, desisted, rested. The Seventh Day became the Sabbath. This is of great significance.

Genesis 2 then goes on to repeat a creation story. Adam and Eve (representing mankind) were created to live in Eden, which means 'pleasure'. We were made to live in a place of harmony, living from the Tree of Life–in other words, sustained eternally by Life that flowed from the Godhead. We were not to become the judge of good and evil (the forbidden tree)–that was God's domain–but to live in total trust of the love and goodness flowing from the Father, Son and Holy Spirit.

The evangelical, revivalist church has often focussed on sin. In fact, this has led to a system of behaviour that identifies sinful actions, even extending to what you drink, how you dress and whether you dance or not! So people are included or excluded based on outward appearance and actions. But as Francois du Toit explains in the Mirror Word, 'sin' derives from two parts, ***ha*** denoting 'not' and ***martia*** denoting 'portion' or 'form'–the identity we were given by God. In other words, sin is really **a basic lack of trust in who God is** and who we were created to be. 'Sins' (plural) are just the fruit of this basic issue. Jesus had no problem with mixing with those struggling with the latter!

The unique quality of Genesis Chapters 1-3 is the personal dimension to the creation account. Unlike some other ancient creation myths, it does not just describe the existence of physical things but the essential relationship of the Creator and creature. After the Fall, when God comes–as, it appears, was his habit–to 'walk in the cool of the evening' with his image-bearer, sharing the joy of a life shared in the kaleidoscope of creation's amazing beauty, he finds Adam and Eve hiding in the bushes! In answer to Adam's lame excuse, 'I hid–I was afraid because I was naked', the Lord gives the ultimate response, 'Who told you ...?' This question echoes through the millennia ... who, apart from God, can tell us who we really are?

The wonder is, however, that from the outset, despite mankind's free choice to launch out on their own, God takes steps towards their redemption. The Father's love never wavered, he never withdrew–it was man who considered himself distant or alienated. The unyielding love of the Father is intent only on healing and restoration. First, man is excluded from a garden in which he would have continued eternally in this broken relationship. Secondly, the Lord graciously covers his sense of shame, by clothing him in animal skins (which some see as a precursor to sacrifice ... ultimately by the Lamb of God). Thirdly, the

Lord prophesies over Eve a time to come when a future offspring–none other than the incarnate Son–will tread the deception underfoot (despite the cost). Hence peace will be restored, and mankind will again dwell in rest. However, there would be many years before this would come about; during this time God is going to slowly reveal to mankind, through story, prophecy and poetry as well as the events of history, the truth about the relationship he has intended from the beginning. The Godhead dwells outside time: so although we dwell in a time-space cosmos, the Lord had made provision in his Son since *'before the foundation of the world'* (Ephesians 1:4).

We were designed for this state of rest. We are hardwired to seek it. However, it cannot be manufactured. I love to sail and enjoy the exhilaration of a good sailing breeze in which my boat will heel over, and–with mainsail and genoa trimmed–will speed along with water over the gunwales, spray flying, through wind power alone. Yet, as exciting as that is, what I treasure above all else are those few days (well, rather few in Scotland) when there is absolutely no wind, and on a mirror-like loch I can glide into a quiet island bay, drop anchor and spend a peaceful night watching the sunset ....

One might think this is the antithesis of the hectic day I described at the outset. It is important to realise, however, true rest *does not* start outside and work in. Of course, the right lifestyle, the right conditions, the right pace of day can all help. But one can live through the first (turbulence and trial) in a state of rest or experience the latter (peaceful surroundings) but lack rest. We can be like the eye of a storm, a person of calm amidst a whirlwind of difficulties. The issue is that the manner of ultimate rest we are discussing is of a different kind, a different source, residing in the heart (the place God refers to as the core of our being). Ultimate rest is holistic with regard to our being. It is this the Gospel addresses: Jesus is that Ultimate Rest.

After the work of Creation, we are told God rested from his labours. The Book of Hebrews refers to this in the context of warning the early Jewish converts that there was no rest outside of God's provision; disobedience was in fact seen as disregarding God's free offer of spiritual rest.

See Hebrews 4:3 in 'The Mirror' paraphrase, with notes in brackets:

> *Faith (not willpower) realizes our immediate access into God's rest. Hear the echo of God's cry through the ages, 'Oh! If only they would enter into my rest.' His rest celebrates perfection. His work is complete; the fall of mankind did not flaw its perfection.* (Sadly most translations read, 'I have sworn in my wrath that they will never enter into my rest.' The word, wrath is derived from *orge,* from ὀρέγομαι *oregomai,* to stretch one's self out in order to touch or to grasp something, to reach after or desire something. The text doesn't say, 'They will never enter my rest.' Both the Septuagint and the Hebrew text quoted here from Psalm 94:11 in the Septuagint, which is Psalm 95:11 in the Hebrew, read, *'Oh that they would enter into my rest.'* Greek *ei* and Hebrew, אִם im. But see Hebrews 4:6, *'It is clear then that there is still an opportunity to enter into that rest...'*)

The writer of Hebrews uses this passage to teach a key point: we were made to live in this place of rest.

The glorious truth is that Jesus *is* our Eternal Sabbath; he is the place of rest we were made for, to live in him, 'hidden in Christ in God'. This is the beautiful, good news of the Gospel. This is why the angels could announce the Incarnation with the words, 'Peace on earth and goodwill to men!'

TWO | The Land

In the desire of the Godhead to reveal their purposes to image-bearers who have 'forgotten the Rock from which they were hewn' (referring to Isaiah 51), they unfold the Truth through the history and culture of mankind. Ironically, God speaks (mainly) through *us*, our histories, our stories, our handed-down accounts, recorded on papyrus and vellum scrolls. To this end, God chooses a particular nation to be *'the womb of the incarnation'*, as Karl Barth put it, deconstructing false, tribal notions about the ways of divinity and unveiling his love and faithfulness. In story after story, illustration after illustration, God gives us a living picture of his nature and his abiding love for mankind. The challenge for us in our day is that he chose to tell this through the eyes and experiences of men and women living initially in a Bronze Age and later a first century Classical era, with all their presumptions and biases. Sometimes events are told through the lens of current understanding, distorting the image we get of God.[3] Nevertheless, through it all, the Holy Spirit shows us the wonder of a God who, when asked by Moses to reveal his glory, reveals only his goodness and compassion for fickle, fragile man.

One of the recurring motifs or themes in the Scriptures is that of the **Land**. God chooses to describe the rest that he has designed us for in terms of a physical country, linking 'man-made-of-soil' with the ground on which he lived. His purpose in this seems to be to

---

[3] This may account for the apparent contradictions we see in certain passages, or mistranslations over the years.

emphasise the physical as well as the ethereal nature of deliverance, freedom, inheritance, provision and wellbeing. He does not do this in ways that are coercive or imposed; rather, the Trinity choose to portray the eternal truths in ways that mankind is invited to respond to. God woos, he does not force us.

A misapprehension about God, commonly held by Christians, is that God controls the universe. However, while he is Sovereign Lord of all creation, he does not control it like clockwork. That Deist view leads to superstition and fatalism. We can fail to grasp the wonder of our existence.

David, after gazing at the Milky Way while tending sheep on the hillsides of Judea, declares in a psalm, *'What is man that you are mindful of him? You have made him a little lower than elohim* (literally 'gods').' (Psalm 8:4-8) God does not control us like puppets. No, the Godhead want a relationship with mankind that is made of the same love and honour that they enjoy. To paraphrase Karl Barth, we may choose to live without God and humanity may prefer a godless existence (indeed, we often do), but God never chooses to live without us. In other words, God wants our participation, that amazingly we might co-reign with him *'seated with him in heavenly places'* (Eph 2:6). In this, we have been created with complete freedom to choose; will we trust the One who formed us in enduring love or break out on our own?

So, the Land becomes a metaphor to teach us the breadth of *shalom* intended for our living environment. About four thousand years ago God spoke to a man called Abram about a promise of this new country, causing him and his family to up sticks and leave what was one of the most sophisticated and advanced cities of that day, Ur of the Chaldees[4]. This man travels with his wife Sara and his relatives, and through various adventures and occurrences, the Lord reveals his intention that '*all* families of the earth will be blessed' by what he is going to bring forth through his dealings with this man and his descendants. This seems impossible, as he and Sara are childless and of advanced age, but God loves to surprise us with seeming impossibilities! As Westerners, we may not appreciate the importance of covenant. However, the implications of God putting Abraham (as he was renamed) into a deep sleep and sovereignly confirming this abiding promise are hugely significant. God was showing that his restoration would come about through divine intent, not man's efforts–a pattern that would be repeated many times over the ensuing centuries.

In one of the precious passages in the Old Testament, Abraham and Sarah receive Three Visitors–surely an encounter with the Holy Trinity–following which the promise of a child is underlined by covenant. Rublev's ikon, now a favourite for many, depicts the Three sitting at table and carries with it such symbolism of the Godhead. In this beautiful image each Person gazes at the other; there is a sense of mutual love and honour. There also appears to be a space at the table, inviting us to join this 'sweet community', though in reality we only do this in Christ ... nevertheless, the intention of our inclusion existed from the beginning.

In due course, against all human odds, Sarah does bear a child. Meanwhile Abraham's ill-conceived dalliance with Hagar effects the

---

[4] In 1927 Leonard Woolley identified Ur Kaśdim with the Sumerian city of Ur (founded c. 3800 BC), in southern Mesopotamia, where the Chaldeans settled much later (around the 9th century BC). The region was considered very wealthy and Ur its chief city.

divergent outcome when mankind tries to resolve the issues of life through human effort, an Ishmael rather than an Isaac. However, God's mercy is seen even in this, in the way each son is treated.

In a moving passage Abraham ascends Mount Moria, with the apparent understanding that he is called to sacrifice Isaac, his first-born son, to Molech and other gods of the ancient world. The thrilling conclusion to this episode is that God stays his hand and draws his attention to a ram caught in a thornbush nearby; Abraham instead sacrifices the sheep and declares that the place will be called 'the Lord will provide'–a beautiful foreshadowing of the provision of the sacrifice-to-end-all-sacrifices when the Son of God will lay down his life. It's as if God is saying, 'If your culture needs a sacrifice, then I will provide it!'[5] Abraham's trust in God is rewarded though: *'I'll bless you–oh, how I'll bless you! And I'll make sure that your children flourish–like stars in the sky! Like sand on the beaches! And your descendants will defeat their enemies. All nations on earth will find themselves blessed through your descendants because you obeyed me.'* (Gen 22:17-18 MSG)

Abraham with his sons and grandsons become very wealthy in the context of their day, with flocks and herds and servants, despite relational disputes and issues as with any other family.

It is later, after the days of Jacob (renamed 'Israel'), that the descendants of Israel find themselves as slaves in Egypt. Again, the Scriptures lay out for us a progression of events that would speak of our own spiritual state through Christ. The Israelites are oppressed

---

[5] The French anthropologist René Girard (1923-2015) identified the scapegoat mechanism as a means by which ancient societies dealt with violence and sought to placate a divine power.

and enslaved to a cruel tyrant, Pharaoh. God raises up a man, Moses, to lead them to freedom. The dramatic scenes are familiar to us, as portrayed in the engaging animation, 'Prince of Egypt'. After an epic struggle Pharaoh eventually agrees to their freedom, only to change his mind and chase after them. Following the Lord's instructions, the Israelites sacrifice a lamb, putting some of the blood on the doorposts of their homes and initiating the Passover meal. God says he will bring *'judgement on all the gods of Egypt'* (Exodus 12:12). He was not against the people, but against the false notions or religious hegemonies they had devised.

As they escape from Egypt, the waters of the Red Sea are parted to allow the Israelites through. These close over however onto Pharaoh's army, providing a clear 'cut-off' from the oppression of their former slave master*: '... of all the Egyptians who had chased the Israelites into the sea, not a single one survived.'* (Exodus 14:28)

God then leads his people across the desert by cloud and fire. The Apostle Paul uses this passage and links it to us when warning about the stupidity of indifference to God's grace in 1 Corinthians 10, saying of the Israelites that *'all of them ate the same spiritual food and all drank the same spiritual water. For they drank from the spiritual rock that travelled with them, and that rock was Christ'.* (NLT) The Holy Trinity were present with them on the journey! As they travel on, God provides for them what they need. He also reveals to Moses a code of ethics (the Law, written on tablets of stone) that was revolutionary in that day. In the ancient world, to limit retaliation to 'an eye for an eye' rather than 'a whole family for an eye' was a huge step forward[6]

[6] Paul Copan makes this case clearly in *Is God a Moral Monster?* (Baker Books, 2011). It was referred to as *lex talionis*, the point being 'the punishment should fit the crime...punishments were to be proportional and couldn't exceed that

–what God is giving them is an incremental change in culture. It has been pointed out that the Ten Commandments are better understood as descriptions of what God's people *shall* be like, rather than a list of dos and don'ts–foreshadowing the full revelation of our identity in Christ.

Deliverance from Egypt was just intended as Part One of the salvation God had for his people. Part Two was to cross the Jordan and enter the land he had provided for them. Yet the story takes a sad turn. When they arrive on the eastern bank, a doubt creeps in, as in the Garden of Eden ... what is it going to be like? Can we trust God's intention in this? So, Moses sends in twelve spies (recorded in Numbers 13). As you may remember, all but two (Joshua and Caleb) return with negative reports: 'Oh! They are like giants there! We were like grasshoppers in their eyes!' They were so deceived as to their true identity that they believed a lie about themselves, even as Adam and Eve had in the Genesis passage. God had said that they would have this Promised Land, but they had filtered that through a human mindset (the Knowledge of Good and Evil) and ended up doubting what was already theirs. So, the result was that they wandered aimlessly in the wilderness for 40 years, until that generation died away. Only Moses' protege Joshua (a name from the same root as Jesus) and the ever-bold Caleb (at over 80 years of age) are left from that original group to enter the land.

The New Testament writer to the Hebrews applies this directly to us, reiterating God's earnest desire that we might live in this state of rest.

---

standard.' This actually protected the weak and vulnerable from the wealthy and powerful.

This is portrayed most clearly in The Mirror paraphrase of Hebrews 4:6-11 by Francois du Toit, who continues:

> *It is clear then that there is still an opportunity to enter into that rest which Israel failed to access because of their unbelief, even though they were the first to hear the Good News of God's intention to restore mankind to the same Sabbath that Adam and Israel had lost. So, now again many years later, he points specifically to an extended opportunity when he announces in David's prophecy, 'Today when hearing my voice, do not do so with a calloused heart. Be faith sensitive.'*
>
> *If Joshua, who led the new generation of Israel out of the wilderness, had succeeded in leading them into the rest that God intended, David would not so many years later have referred to yet another day.* (This moment still remains as an open invitation to mankind to enter into their rest: the living blueprint of their design. This confirms that the history of Israel was a mere shadow and prophetic type of that Promise that was yet to be fulfilled.)
>
> *The conclusion is clear: the original rest is still in place for God's people. God's rest celebrates his finished work; whoever enters into God's rest immediately abandons his own efforts to improve what God has already perfected. Let us therefore be prompt to understand and fully appropriate that rest and not fall again into the same trap that snared Israel in unbelief.*

It is spelled out so clearly for us: Jesus *is* our Promised Land, he *is* our Sabbath rest! How many of us, in confused, deluded humanity, wander aimlessly through lives of empty wilderness, when God has already provided an abundant, safe, thrilling Land of wide-open spaces for us to enjoy and explore? The delightful discovery open to all of us is that this is not far off, beyond our reach. It is already 'at hand': a Land/Kingdom that we may dwell in today. In fact, we are already included in the inheritance that our Joshua/Jesus has led us into!

No one chooses where or to whom they are born. To some born in a prosperous country, their 'accident of birth' confers on them great privilege while to others born in less fortunate lands, they may find themselves with extreme challenges. Those rendered stateless by political upheaval or becoming refugees are in a particular predicament. Nevertheless, none of us essentially choose this, it is conferred upon us. We are all, however, made in the image of God and in that sense share a common humanity in Christ through whom all things are created and held. The world-system would place us in *'Self-Effortania'*, leading to our striving for acceptance due to Adam's deception and our ensuing choices. But the stunning truth is that through the vicarious work of the Last Adam, Jesus Christ, we have been transferred to a new home we could call *'Grace-Land'*. All the benefits of that country apply to us! This is no accident of birth; we are *'born from above'* into a new state through the will and intention of the Godhead, who never desired that we would live anywhere else. *'While we were yet sinners Christ died for us...'* (Rom 5:8) The amazing grace of God is that he overcame every obstacle in order that we should know the healing and wholeness of the Kingdom of God. Distance, separation and delay have been dealt with through the passionate love of the Lover of our Souls.

THREE | What then is rest?

Sometimes it is easier to understand the mysteries of the Kingdom of God by describing what they are not, as in the apophatic descriptions of God (the knowledge of him obtained through saying what he is not). The 'rest' we are describing is not laziness, atrophy or boredom. It is not indifference or apathy regarding God and his ways, or to mankind or the planet. It is not giving up, or necessarily just lying back in a deckchair and falling asleep (though both of these may be entirely appropriate)!

Rest is directly linked to the grace of God. Grace is at the heart of the Gospel. However, religious-minded people quickly become wary of an over-emphasis on grace. They introduce a 'but ....' when grace is promoted: 'but God is also holy .... but God is just .... but God also judges ....' as if somehow there needed to be bumpers put down the Gospel bowling alley to keep us from falling into the gutter. But it is not up to us to don the correct footwear, perfect our aim and propel the heavy black bowl down the centre of the ten-pin track in order to know God's approval and love. The grace of God is that Jesus has already made the perfect strike! We get to celebrate in his winning score!

So, rest is in essence a state of spiritual ease and all-encompassing assurance (affecting our whole being: body, mind and emotions), enjoyed through a total dependence on Christ and his work. It is holistic–not about advancing to a higher, spiritual plane as Eastern Mysticism would often suggest–rather it is living here and now, in the grittiness of earthly, human life in union with Christ *'who is our righteousness, who is our life'* [Col 3:4]. In a sense, it *is* about 'giving up'... giving up on any of our own efforts:

> The gospel of grace is the end of religion, the final posting of the CLOSED sign on the sweatshop of the human race's perpetual struggle to think well of itself. For that, at bottom, is what religion is: man's well-meant but dim-witted attempt to approve of his unapprovable condition by doing odd jobs he thinks some important Something will thank him for. Religion, therefore, is a loser, a strictly fallen activity. It has a failed past and a bankrupt future. There was no religion in Eden and there won't be any in heaven; and in the meantime, Jesus has died and risen to persuade us to knock it all off right now. (Robert F. Capon)[7]

In Romans 13:14 Paul encourages the believers: 'put on' or 'clothe' yourselves with Christ. He uses a Greek word *enduo,* meaning in effect to 'sink into' as one would sink into a garment. Imagine yourself sinking into a warm puffed-out coat on a cold winter day–it envelopes you and protects you from the freezing temperatures.

As a child of about 6 years of age I used to travel with my great-aunt to visit my grandmother and her companion, who lived in a large old house in Erdington, Birmingham UK. I remember at that time I would attempt to sing early Beatles numbers like, 'She loves you, yeah, yeah, yeah'... and probably wore out my elderly relatives with my enthusiasm ... so, much to my chagrin, I was required to have a 'rest' every afternoon in the spare room upstairs. Here my grandmother's friend had a bed covered with, what seemed to me at the time, a

---

[7] Robert F. Capon, *Between Noon and Three* (Wm. B. Eerdmans, 1997).

voluminous feather mattress. As I climbed into its soft mounds and lay back I would *enduo*–sink down into–its comfortable, spongy mass. It was actually easy to rest there. Years later the Lord reminded me of this; I did not need to 'do' anything to enter his presence, there were no hoops to jump through, I only had to 'sink into' the Lord Jesus Christ and know his encompassing sufficiency.

A song by Godfrey Birtill captures the sense of this so eloquently:

> I'm sinking into Jesus
> I'm falling into these robes
>
> Into His garment of compassion
> His garment of longsuffering
> His garment of patience
> His garment of grace
> Into his tender-hearted mercy
> His clothing of meekness
> His clothing of kindness, His clothing of love
>
> We are living, we are living,
> We are living, in love.
>
> I'm sinking into Jesus
> I'm falling into these robes
>
> Into His garment of refreshment
> His garment of freedom
> His garment of resting
> His garment of joy
> A peace beyond all understanding

His clothing of wonders
His clothing of goodness, this clothing of God

I'm in love, I'm in Christ
I am a new creation living a new life.
Clothed in Christ, clothed in Christ, clothed in Christ Jesus.[8]

We have so often presented to new believers an idea that Christ has 'got us started' but now we need to progress through stages of holiness, to sanctify ourselves so that we can be near God. This may have been described like going through the courts of the temple–approaching with due caution because of his holiness–or like progressing up a mountain, slowly attaining greater heights of purification. This misses entirely the wonder of the Gospel, that through no effort or merit of our own we have been *made new*; in fact, we have been co-crucified with Christ and also co-raised with him. It was a transformation! We are born as children of the Light and *'shine like bright stars' (Phil 2:15)*. Thus, we are described as saints, holy ones, set apart through his redeeming work.

This does not negate the fact that we are to mature as we walk with him, in him, through life. Or that we retain free will and can–if we want to be stupid–ignore the ways of God and do our own thing still. But as we grow in understanding, so increasingly the way of our being aligns with the truth of our being, which is that we are made in the image of God to share in the divine life–living each day in the overflow of the joy of the Trinity!

---

[8] Godfrey & Gill Birtill (Thankyou Music, UK) © available on the album *The Wine is Alive*, 2011. Godfrey Birtill has been foremost in conveying the gospel of grace in recent years.

God is described to us both as love and as perfect light. Scientific discovery indicates to us that the smallest building blocks of the universe are made of light. Quantum physics has revealed an intriguing connection between the particles at the core of all things, that conceivably show us an aspect of how all things are *'held in Christ'*. Nothing exists outside of Him ... *'we all breathe Christological air'*, to quote Baxter Kruger.

It should not come as a surprise to us then that Jesus' appeal, when walking this earth among a people who were mired in legalism and religious observance, should be, *'Come to me, all you who are heavy laden, and I will give you* ***rest****.'* (Matthew 11:28 NIV) Judaism had added numerous rules and requirements to the law. Like a pernicious weed in the garden, the religious spirit grew deep roots, and spawned runners in all directions to spread its influence. But the free gift of Life cannot be upgraded or improved ... new wine needs new wineskins! Jesus' invitation, recorded through Matthew, is to be yoked to him–we are united with him through his amazing work–and learn of his ways (our true identity, a mirror of who we really are now). His nature is not critical, punitive or driven; we learn from him because he *'is gentle and humble in heart, and you will find rest for your souls'* (Matt 11:29-30). A yoke joins two, so they act as one.

Brian Simmons translates this from the Aramaic as, *'Come to me. I will refresh your life, for I am your oasis'*, and the word 'gentle' as 'tranquil' or 'peaceful'. For *'all I require of you will be pleasant ['kind' or 'delightful'] and easy to bear'* (TPT).

In the next passage in Matthew, Jesus is walking with his disciples through a field of wheat on the Sabbath. You can imagine the scene: it was a typically hot Middle Eastern afternoon; they had been with the Lord among the crowds as he had shared some parables of the Kingdom. They were probably having a quieter day, but as they went outside a village, they strolled through some of the cultivation at the edge. They were hungry, so were snacking on the heads of grain. But the religious mindset immediately finds fault, so the Pharisees take issue. (How often even today religious people will look to find fault with those who seem to be relaxed, who are enjoying just hanging out in company with Jesus!). Jesus responds though and reframes the argument, reminding them of how David even entered the holy place and ate the sacred bread of the Presence: 'I'm greater than the Sabbath, or the temple'–we should understand, the Holy of Holies is now here, within us! We love to overcomplicate this relationship with the Lover of our Souls. This is intended to be our return to Eden [lit. 'pleasure'] as we participate in the most exciting life available to mankind, the Life of Mr Pleasure living within us.

> *The son of man is not the slave of the Sabbath, he is Master of the Sabbath.*
>
> (... The Sabbath of God points to his perfect work of both revealing and redeeming his image and likeness in human form. Every Sabbath continues to celebrate the perfection of our Father's work - until now! So when Jesus heals people on the Sabbath he is not contradicting it, but endorsing it. Jesus is what the Sabbath is all about! He is the substance of every prophetic shadow. In restoring someone's wholeness, the idea of the original Sabbath is reinforced and not compromised. When God introduced the Sabbath it was always meant to be a prophetic opportunity to celebrate his Rest, which was him seeing his perfect work unveiled in us. He continues to invite us to enter into his Rest where we cease from our own works.

> The announcement, 'You shall do NO WORK!' was to remind us again and again that his work is perfect, and we cannot improve on it! You cannot improve on you! You are his workmanship - his masterpiece! The deadly fruit of the 'I am not ...' tree-system had to be thoroughly uprooted!) Luke 6:5 (MIR)

The Creation account could not be clearer in presenting two options, two mindsets, two sources: the two trees may grow in the centre of the same garden but are polar opposites for humanity.

The Tree of the Knowledge of Good and Evil has been likened to the world's system, the efforts of man to solve the issues of existence by purely human endeavour. To make judgements on right and wrong in a way that was not about darkness and light, but about the subtle benefit they give our own egos–a man-centred rather than God-centred understanding. To seek to appropriate 'goodness' through performance or religious observance. To build trade systems that exploit, that benefit the privileged at the expense of the many. To wage war and dominate others, to impose a culture (or even Christendom) on those considered weaker or backward. The fruit on this tree looks so appealing at times, so juicy and easy to pick! 'Why would God not want you to eat that–does he want to stop you becoming like him?', the counter narrative goes. But to eat from this tree, God gives a clear and unequivocal NO! 'To eat from that tree will be the death of you! Choose life!'

The other tree, the Tree of Life flourishes nearby. This is the provider from a Life Source that will eternally sustain mankind in thriving harmony and resonance with the Godhead. The man and the woman were being tempted to choose another path that would somehow better their lot, make them more powerful, more successful, more able to get on well on this planet ... for surely, the lie goes, the Trinity are somehow keeping something from you? Of course, the truth was actually that they had *already* been created in the image of God, they were already made to share in the Divine Life.

Jesus faced the same counter narrative for us when he went into the desert for 40 days. 'Choose another path, you don't have to trust the Father, you can just take it for yourself now!' He did not fall for the subtle lie, and as an example of us (the Last Adam) he refuted the *satanus* deceit–which would be cast down forever on the cross. *'The time for judging this world has come, when Satan, the ruler of this world, will be cast out. And when I am lifted up from the earth, I will draw everyone to myself.'* (John 12:31-32) He taught us instead how we were made to live from the same source of life as he did, incarnate and experiencing all the challenges of living as we do. This Tree of Life was also the True Vine that we belong in: as we live from that source, he produces abundant fruit through our lives. No branch was ever able to produce its own fruit; the crop depended entirely upon the life-flowing sap from the root and stem.

The Tree of Life was depicted in a striking manner in a contemporary stained-glass window by Roger Wagner at St Michael's, Iffley near Oxford, England. In this powerful image, Christ is shown on the Cross superimposed on the Tree; his vicarious work is the Tree of Life for us, as we live from this Eternal Source. The artist shows the River of Life flowing from the foot of the Tree, with animals and birds on its grassy banks. We understand from Colossians that all things are created through, and held in place by, the Son of God. It is not surprising then that the work he did–from the incarnation, through to the passion, the resurrection and ascension–is fundamental to the well-being of the cosmos. Seen by the prophet Ezekiel (Chapter 47) and then revealed for us in the closing chapters of the remarkable Book of Revelation, this River of Life brings healing and vitality to all.

The Gospel message is that we, like the thief on the cross beside Jesus, need only to look at him–trusting in who he is–to benefit from this vicarious act (which we are already included in). *'Today you will be with me in paradise'* (Luke 23:43) Consider how when in former times, through defiance, the Children of Israel were wandering in the desert, infested by snakes and suffering from their poisonous bites. Moses was told by God to make a bronze serpent and put it up on a pole (Numbers 21:8-9). All the afflicted had to do was look up at that and they were healed! Jesus refers to this passage and links it directly to what he came to do in John 3:14 *'And as Moses lifted up the bronze snake on a pole in the wilderness, so the Son of Man must be lifted up'*. The word for 'salvation' (*sozo* GK.) is a holistic word meaning wholeness: healed, restored, delivered and preserved. We 'bring nothing to the table' to this end; it is the faith *of* Christ (or *the faithfulness of* Christ) that has achieved this happy state. All we can do is gaze on his finished work with astonishment and gratitude.

FOUR | Operating out of rest

What I am describing is a mind-shift, a *metanoia* (the Greek word traditionally translated as repentance, which actually refers to having a different mindset[9]) that comes with fully receiving the Gospel, with all its implications. Beatrice Bruteau says it is best understood like an iOS upgrade on your computer: your whole way of operating has been changed. Jesus came to give us life and give it abundantly. But he did not come as an example for us to follow–the world has had enough gurus who teach that–rather he came to give us HIS life. He came as an example not for us, but of us.[10]

What about all the instructions in his teaching? What about all the injunctions in the Gospels? Were these given as a new set of rules to replace those in the Old Testament? In fact it is clear that they raise the bar to an incredible level (even a wrong thought or unclean glance is "for the fire"). No, Jesus is showing us that, even on our best day, we could never, ever meet the standard of righteousness that would be required for heaven's kingdom. What to do? Only to trust fully in his righteousness, 'die' with him on the cross and be born from above as a New Creation. Jesus and the writers of the New Testament are describing to us what this life in harmony with the Godhead looks like.

---

[9] Consider the Greek word μετάνοια metanoia, from meta, together with, and noieō, to perceive with the mind; which describes the awakening of the mind to that which is true; a re-alignment of one's reasoning; it is a gathering of one's thoughts, a co-knowing. (Francois du Toit in the introduction to The Mirror Bible).

[10] Ibid.

Of course, obedience to God's ways is important, but who could be 100% obedient? Only Christ, who by his obedience and faithfulness we now have life.

> *For through the law I died to the law, so that I might live to God. My old identity has been co-crucified with Christ and no longer lives. And now the essence of this new life is no longer mine, for the Anointed One lives his life through me—we live in union as one! My new life is empowered by the faith of the Son of God who loves me so much that he gave himself for me, dispensing his life into mine!* (Galatians 2:19-20 TPT)

The glorious revelation is that we start from this place of Rest, this place of peace and righteousness. As Francois du Toit states, any ideas of separation or distance are cancelled at the cross. We are now included in Christ–he is our righteousness–and we participate in the life of the Godhead.

The Orthodox Church teach us much about this in their understanding of *theosis*: sharing in the divine life. It may be beyond our comprehension that we can share this life of the Godhead, but that is exactly the Father's intention. We should not overthink it, rather trust in the life-flow that is ours through the Son of God. It may mean that we may need to revise some of our ideas about who we are now, though. Healing, miracles, mystical union–none of these come from us–yet there is no limit to what is available in God. We do not acquire these attributes though dogged perseverance either; we rather acquaint ourselves with our true likeness in Christ. The Holy Spirit loves to teach us of these things.

When we consider the accounts of Jesus in the Gospels, we get so many insights into how he operated from a place of rest. The scene for this is set at his baptism, when he has the wonderful affirmation from the Father, *'This is my Son in whom I'm well pleased.'* This assurance sets the tone for his ministry! When the crowds turn angry in Nazareth and threaten to throw him off a cliff, he calmly walks through them. When people press in on all sides, he quietly turns and addresses the woman with the persistent medical problem, 'Who has touched my cloak?" When his house meeting is disrupted by people breaking through the roof above–straw and clay, sticks and stones showering like confetti on the gathered audience below–they lower someone down before him so that their friend could get healed. He calmly addresses both the paralysed man–healing him–and reveals the inner thoughts of his detractors. When travelling with the disciples, followed by thronging masses who all demand signs and wonders, he just keeps in step with the Father. He often goes off to spend time quietly in conversation with him, to confirm what he is doing is in harmony with heaven. He tells the disciples to *'Come aside and rest awhile'* after a particularly busy period. When he's in the boat on the Sea of Galilee with them and a storm blows up, he is not stressed or concerned; in fact, he is a picture of rest, asleep on a cushion at the stern! When awoken by his distressed friends, he just speaks a word of command to still the waves and then uses their experience as a teaching moment.

His relationship with two sisters and their brother at Bethany is remarkable. When Mary sits at his feet, he does not condemn Martha for her preparations–which are surely needed for any meal–but highlights the life-source that her sister is feeding from. When sometime later their brother falls ill, Jesus does not react to the external circumstances–the urgency, the shock, the fear–but waits until he knows he should come to them. 'If you'd only been here my brother would not have died!' Martha wails. Jesus is fully in touch with his emotions–he weeps with them–but then calmly, authoritatively addresses Lazarus' corpse and commands him to rise from his tomb!

In the days leading up to his Passion, he's not rushed by his siblings who say, 'Now is the time you should be going to the feast; show what you can do!' Instead, he travels up to Jerusalem when he knows the time is right with the Father, and then preaches to the crowds. At a time when he would have been aware the days were counting down to his arrest and crucifixion, he travels around Jerusalem speaking to the crowds openly in the temple courts. Yet even when the tension is mounting, he takes time out to join 'a meal held in his honour' in nearby Bethany by the ever-hospitable Martha (a meal which his friend Lazarus is now delighted to attend)!

When the moment of his arrest finally arrives, he faces it confident in his Father's will. His time in Gethsemane must have been one of the hardest up to that point, with the weight of the world's sin bearing down on him, the capillaries on his brow breaking open with blood as the intensity of the situation crowded in.[11] But when he enters the Kidron Valley with his disciples, and is confronted by a whole cohort of guards and betrayed by one of his own, he says, 'Leave these others, it's me you want,' and permits them to bind him and take him away. Dragged before the high priest, then Herod and Pilate, when threatened with crucifixion, he answers the Roman Consul from the same place of rest he has been in throughout: 'Do you not think I

[11] A rare condition known as Hematidrosis is when great stress causes excretion of blood or blood pigment in the sweat. Dr Luke records this medical detail in his Gospel account.

could command a legion of angels to come to my rescue? You would not have any power over me unless it had been given you'. He does not react, retaliate or condemn those who scourge and eventually crucify him–with probably the worst form of torture and humiliating execution devised by fallen mankind–but calmly endures the suffering, 'drinking the pain and wrongdoing of humanity to its dregs'. 'It is finished!' he declares, while with the ultimate humility and love of God, says, 'Father forgive them, they don't know what they do.'

T.F. Torrance emphasised how we are saved by the *whole* of Christ's work; his very incarnation was a vital aspect of our redemption, for in this vicarious act he both lived our life and died our death. He identified with us in every way so that, through our mystical union with him, we might live out of his victory. Thus, it does not 'fall back on us' but rather we live from his life, his sufficiency, his fulness.

When we approach the traditional areas of the Christian life such as prayer, worship, prophecy, evangelism, guidance etc, how often have we allowed stress or pressure to be our pace setter, or been motivated by a misplaced sense of expectation or religious obligation? How important it is, rather, that we live from this same place of rest ... his rest. This is the healthy Christian life.

> What I have observed so often in the Christian Church is that whether conservative or liberal, traditional or contemporary, emergent or mega-church, Christians basically live as if saved by grace but sanctified by works. We depend on our own efforts, choices, accomplishments or zeal. Grace is where we start the Christian life but often we somehow end up 'thrown back upon our own resources' and feeling under a great burden. Then we become first unimpressed, then perhaps

depressed, and finally even coldly cynical about the whole Christian life itself.[12]

Understanding that the Christian life is an unpacking, a discovering, an adventure in the wonder of who we *are* now in union with Christ, takes the pressure off us to perform and frees us to run with joyful abandon. It does not make us lazy–Paul was a passionate preacher of the Gospel for 'the love of Christ constrains us' (2 Cor 5:14).

Prayer is clearly a central aspect of our faith, yet how often we have made it into another work? We recognise that so many men and women of great depth have trodden this path over the centuries, and we can sit at their feet to learn, yet it is sometimes the case that we can feel overwhelmed by the pressure 'Have we prayed enough?' Some intercessors become very 'burdened', searching for hidden keys to unlock situations or historical injustices to repent for.[13] Do we see St Paul and the other apostles approaching prayer like that?

Prayer and worship can become like a hamster wheel that we keep working at. Nevertheless, it's more helpful if we see prayer rather as an overflow of the victory already achieved in Christ. We cannot do more than God has already done in Jesus! Instead, Paul writes of Christ leading a victory procession (2 Cor 2:14) as rulers would do in the ancient world to demonstrate their total vanquishing of their enemies. We should therefore take a stance of simply 'abiding' in this victory. We do not need to help him out by entering a dualistic war in which the enemy may get the upper hand if we don't do our part.

---

[12] Deddo *The Christian Life* p.138-9 quoted by Alexandra Sophie Radcliff in *The Claim of Humanity in Christ* (Princeton, 2016), 123-4.

[13] Benni Johnson wrote *The Happy Intercessor* (Destiny Image Publishers, 2013) to counter this image.

None of this is to deny the importance of prayer (*'Prayer is an ongoing conversation; praying in the spirit includes every form of prayer, whether it be a prayer of request or a prayer of thanksgiving, or worship or interceding for all to realize their saintly innocence. Oh, and remember, you do not have to do all the talking. Always be attentive to the voice of the Spirit.'* Eph 6:18 MIRROR); rather, see it as an aspect of our union, an ongoing conversation with the Godhead. In fact, our whole lives can be seen as prayer, flowing from a place of rest.

It has been said that the Mystics understood God saying, 'Pray without ceasing' as 'Rest in me.' It can be a very quiet, contemplative act, often without words. It is primarily about relationship; when people are very close, they will often just enjoy time silently together. Theophan the Recluse wrote, 'To pray is to descend with the mind into the heart, and there to stand before the face of the Lord, ever present, all seeing, within you.' He also said, 'Prayer is standing in the Presence of God with the mind in the heart; that is then at the point of our being where there are no divisions or distinctions and where we are totally one. There God's Spirit dwells and there the great encounter takes place. There heart speaks to heart because we stand before the face of the Lord, all seeing within us.'

Of course, there are times to be specific in praying for people or situations. Something we have been exploring is the way that, when we see something done through Jesus–we like to term it 'Seeing Prayer', we align with heaven's perspective, heaven's rhythms, and things change. Jesus spoke of it like this: *'Have faith in God. I tell you the truth, you can say to this mountain, "May you be lifted up and thrown into the sea," and it will happen. But you must really believe it will happen and have no doubt. I tell you, you can pray for anything, and if you believe that you've received it, it will be yours....'* (Mark 11:23-24 NLT) Jesus spoke of prayer as going into the 'inner room', that secret place deep within, where we sense the rhythm of heaven, and see situations aligning with that. There is something profound here about who we are, as much loved, adopted children–those sharing in the Divine life–that Romans 8 tells us all creation is waiting to see arise.

Similarly with worship, we do not need to take the stance of someone in the Old Covenant, who had to approach through the outer courts, bringing offerings and sacrifices in order to make themselves acceptable to a holy God. They were reliant on a priest to make the necessary oblation on their behalf. No, we have a High Priest who has entered the holy place for us. In fact he has torn the temple curtain from top to bottom that separated us, indeed he *is* the perfect lamb, he *is* the mercy seat, he *is* the Holy Place in whom we now dwell! So, our songs do not need now to implore him to come–he *has come*–or ask him to make us clean–he *has made us righteous* through his full and sufficient work. Rather we can sing with the overflowing praises of those living in his abundance, his inheritance, 'seated with him in heavenly places.' As John Crowder states, warfare then becomes 'joyfare' as we sing of these truths.

Prophecy is a wonderful gift which can really encourage, strengthen and build up (1 Cor 14:3). It is most healthy though when interwoven into the life of the community rather than set on a platform, like some sort of show. It does not need to be forced. We can fall into a trap however of making it like hidden knowledge, a gnostic approach where those 'in the know' give privileged insight to enquirers. The Lord is always speaking–he gives us direction and confirmation– but this is not to show us some, as yet undisclosed, new plan around the corner or a new season with a different approach ... Jesus *is* the new thing, he *is* the new season! This does not deny that there may well be new depths of understanding, new facets, that the Lord opens up to us through dreams or other prophetic revelation, but these are all found in Christ.

Evangelism is one area that has been much misunderstood and led to extremes; either total absence as people feel unable or inhibited to say anything about their faith, or an intense 'scalps on the belt' approach to making converts, that is forced and often exhausting. But we forget, it is the Lord's delight to awaken those who are asleep to the wonder of the Gospel. The Holy Spirit is at work everywhere, we are just participating in the family business. We read in Ephesians 1:4 *'Even before he made the world, God loved us and chose us in Christ to be holy and without fault in his eyes.'* And in 2 Timothy 1:9 that *'He gave us resurrection life and drew us to himself by his holy calling on our lives. And it wasn't because of any good we have done, but by his divine pleasure and marvellous grace that confirmed our union with the anointed Jesus, even before time began!'* So, we know he has, a) already made up his mind about mankind before anything existed and, b) made full and sufficient provision through his Son, the Last Adam: *'For as in Adam all die, so also in Christ shall all be made alive.'* (1 Corinthians 15:22 NASB)

When, with a Trinitarian perspective, we see that everything has been created in Christ from the outset, and held together in him, we know therefore that no one is really separate from him (except in their own minds–'enemies in their minds'). In fact, people are only considered lost because they once belonged. So, we don't need to view people as 'other' or 'outsiders'–rather, as those who have not yet grasped or awakened to the wonderful truth of their redemption. After all, Jesus is the Saviour of the World (lit. *cosmos* Gk.). We can approach evangelism from a place of rest, as joyful heralds of good news. No need to force it; just flow with the Father, Son and Holy Spirit in their love for their creation and mankind. We can 'gossip the gospel' in the midst of healthy, non-religious lives lived from a place of rest, displaying peace and hope, authentically demonstrating what has been accomplished on our behalf. Yet we *do* have a message to bring to a hurting world that still tries to feed from the wrong tree. If we don't do it, who will? 'The essential nature of the church is the fellowship of the astonished heart.' [14] We share our wonder at the revelation of Christ within us.

For example, we live in a converted Victorian church building and from time to time get various people ringing our doorbell with requests for help. A woman rang the bell and asked for some money for food. She appeared somewhat harassed and appeared to be from a travelling community who pass through occasionally. I felt it was wiser to give a bag of food rather than money, but as I chatted to her, I felt overwhelmed with the love that the Godhead had for this 'daughter of Eve'. Not feeling the pressure to 'convert' her, I nevertheless just spoke to her of how special she was, how she was created by one who has always loved her from before the beginning of time. By the time she left, her face was beaming.

Similarly, our Community has in the past gathered in the local coffee shop advertising an evening called 'Spirit Rhythms'. We provided some live instrumental music and had various tables offering prayer for healing, spiritual insights or dream interpretation etc. It was a

---

[14] Dr. Baxter Kruger, in conversation, quoted by this author in *Reconstructing Ecclesia* (Amazon, 2022), 8

delight to give encouragement to people, speaking to 'the treasure within', regardless of who they were or how they presented themselves.

People sometimes approach guidance as if there is a hidden, precise blueprint for their lives, and they feel under great pressure to fast and pray in order to discover it. God is seen as some great controller of all things, and if they step out of line they will fall out of favour and miss his will. But this is a deist approach, that sees the universe running like clockwork, a 'grim determinism, which is fatalism without personality.'[15] We are not puppets–we are a much higher order of creation than that! We have been made in God's image 'a little lower than *Elohim*'[16] with incredible freedom, creativity and spiritual as well as physical power. We have been created because the Godhead desired to share their flow of dynamic, other-centred, love-saturated life beyond themselves, so all things were created in and through Christ, in order that we may participate in this together. We turned away from the light as those born in the first Adam, but through the amazing grace of God have now been wonderfully restored in the Last Adam, Jesus Christ, to experience this union again. So, guidance is more like the family weaving a beautiful, intricately patterned Persian carpet. The Father knows fully the splendour the finished piece will carry, but if one of the children drop a stitch or make a mistake, he does not abandon what they are doing, he just changes the pattern so that the carpet may be continued. There is mystery here as we consider the unfolding of time and events, which we will probably

---

[15] Wm. Paul Young emphasises this point in his book *Lies we believe about God* (Simon & Schuster, 2017), 37-38, noting 'Control does not originate in God, but submission does.'

[16] The Hebrew text of Psalm 8 refers to man being made a little lower than *Elohim* (God), a word which can also mean mighty angels.

never grasp until the consummation of all things, but we are clearly designed to rest in God 'who works out all things for good' (Rom 8:28).

God does guide us; many will recognise the sense of peace that accompanies a decision, or the absence of that if the choice is unwise, or maybe not for now. But at times feelings and a sense of direction can be hard to discern. We can then simply trust, resting in the assurance that we are in Christ and he is in us, and not getting tied in knots trying to predict the outcome. We already have his favour–don't try to earn what he has already given. His voice is saying over *you*, 'This is my son/daughter in whom I'm well pleased!' Ultimately, his will for our lives is that we live in union with him–we do not need to over-complicate this.

Many have taught on the five-fold ministry and the different gifts and ways of service in the church. Most have had the best intentions and a genuine desire to see the Kingdom expressed, and we can honour the contribution they have made over the decades. However, we seem to be entering another time of reformation in the *Ecclesia* in which many of these areas are ripe for reimagining. Some approaches in 'charismania' have fed easily into hierarchical or controlling structures which have thrived for a while but ignored their eventual effects on people. Who has heard of pastors or worship leaders who have been burnt out, or risen in a system only to fall out of favour and be spat out and rejected at some later stage?

This is an important, separate discussion[17] but should not lead us to reject *Ecclesia* or the purpose for which the Lord brought the church into being. Rather, this should send up red flags for aspects that have been born out of striving or misinterpretation. There is an abundant flow of life from the Tree of Life, the Trinitarian Lord of Glory, that he wants us to rest in as we participate with him in the unveiling of his Kingdom on earth!

---

[17] I discuss the changing nature of church in *Reconstructing Ecclesia* (Wellsprings Community, Amazon 2023).

FIVE | Participation

When we consider the wonder of the Gospel, there are so many facets that shine with God's incredible, pure light. In fact, we could say that Ultimate Love is at the heart of this message, as God is love and he demonstrated this for all time through becoming man–taking on the very dust of the stars and planets he has created–entering our darkness and redeeming us 'from the inside'. As emphasised in the preceding chapters, his intention is that we therefore **rest** in his Finished Work, and that everything we go on to do from now on flows from this place of rest. So many of us have been taught a transactional gospel, when instead what God is presenting to us is a gospel of a relationship restored, of adoption, of participation. Yes, we were dead in our sins (unbelief) but we were rescued by the Lover of our Souls. The *telos* (culmination) of this gospel is that we live in union with the Son and participate in the divine life of the Godhead. Athanasius wrote, *'God in Christ became the bearer of flesh for a time in order that man could become the bearer of Spirit forever.'* He is not a distant Being that we must implore to meet with us; he is ever present, the very air we breathe, the environment we dwell in.

> Jesus is not up there in some celestial sanctuary waiting for us to get our act together. He has not vacated the premises and left us as orphans, outside the circle of his family life. He is not absent, he is present. And the one who is present is the incarnate Son, who shares all life and all glory and all fullness and all joy with his Father in the fellowship of the Spirit. The one who is present is the incarnate Son, the New Man who is face to face with the Father; the Victor, who lives beyond evil

> and darkness; the Covenant Man, who lives in unhindered fellowship with the Father. The mystery at work in the universe, the light of life, the secret, is that Jesus Christ is already sharing his life with us. The great dance is afoot in your life and mine.[18]

We were designed to participate with the Father, Son and Holy Spirit (who, it has been noted by Baxter Kruger, never travel separately) in this union, this oneness. We don't become God–we are still distinct as his created beings–yet amazingly we are intended for *theosis* (to share in the divine nature and participate in the life of God). The Apostle Peter encapsulated this in his letter: 2 Peter 1:3-4

> *By his divine power, God has given us everything we need for living a godly life. We have received all of this by coming to know him, the one who called us to himself by means of his marvellous glory and excellence. And because of his glory and excellence, he has given us great and precious promises. These are the promises that enable you to share his divine nature and escape the world's corruption caused by human desires.* (NLT)

> *By his divine engineering he gifted us with all that it takes to live life to the full, where our ordinary day to day lives mirror our devotion and romance with our Maker. His intimate knowledge of us introduces us to ourselves again and elevates us to a position where his original intention is clearly perceived.*

---

[18] Dr Baxter Kruger, *The Great Dance* (Regent College Publishing, 2000), 53

> *This is exactly what God always had in mind for us; every one of his abundant and priceless promises pointed to our restored participation in our godly origin. This is his gift to us. In this fellowship we have escaped the distorted influence of the corrupt cosmic virus of greed.* (MIR)

We may initially balk at the idea that we can share the divine nature, feeling that it may be arrogant or claiming equality with God. This is a misunderstanding though; of course, we are still created beings, but this perspective actually honours the incarnation and work of Christ in bringing us into union. This was in the heart of the Triune God from before time began! It can only be described as 'mystical union'–the unveiling of the mystery of the grace of God in our lives. *'You are plunging into the never-ending joy of discovery. Discovering the glorious gift that has been deposited within you. Christian growth and maturity is about discovering the True Self, not becoming it.'*[19] We were made in the image of God–in Christ Jesus his image and likeness is redeemed in us. It as if the default settings are restored; we are rebooted to fully participate in the *'life of our design'*. *Theosis 'is perfect harmony, perfect rest'*[20] as we are reminded who we really are. Athanasius wrote, *'For that was the very purpose and end of our Lord's incarnation that he should join what is man by nature to Him who is by nature God'*.

Brother Lawrence is a 17th Century friar who brought us such insight into this life of rest in his letters and writings, later published as *The Practice of the Presence of God*. He was not from a privileged background and had returned, injured and traumatised from serving

---

[19] John Crowder, *Mystical Union* (Sons of Thunder Ministries & Publications, 2010). He unpacks the wonder of who we are now in Christ with great clarity.
[20] Dr Shawn Smith teaching online about *Theosis*.

as a soldier in the appalling Thirty Years War. He went through some difficult times, yet in joining a monastery and serving others by working in the kitchen, he developed an exceptional understanding of resting in God. He spoke of presence as the constant awareness of God, something we *'become accustomed to'* in how we position ourselves as with developing a habit, yet coming from the heart rather than from the mind. To him, it was a total awareness of God's love for him, an ensuing calmness, and a love for others. He did not imply practicing was to become a 'work' but rather an intention, a state of being. He valued simplicity, even in his monastic setting, and avoiding over-analysis. He even said, *'Overthinking is the source of the world's problems'*[21]– that was his view around 350 years ago, yet so relevant in our complex, high-octane world today!

Despite his humble view of himself and his shortcomings, he writes regarding his relationship with God, *'This King, full of mercy and goodness, very far from chastising me, embraces me with love, makes me eat at his table, serves me with his own hands, gives me the key of his treasures; he converses and delights himself with me incessantly, in a thousand and a thousand ways, and treats me in all respects as his favourite. It is thus I consider myself from time to time in his holy presence.'* This attitude of being included–actually a *favourite*–at the Lord's abundant feast is so helpful. We are all his favourites, and we need to remember that at the 'Wedding feast of the Lamb' we are included not just as a minor guest, some distant cousin on a side table, seated behind a pillar, but as the Bride, the object of his affection. That is why Jesus died and rose again for you ... because he

[21] Quoted by Carmen Avevido Butcher, who recently translated his works, speaking on the Nomad podcast, 2023.

loves you and wanted you included. The Godhead have wanted us included from the start.

Brother Lawrence takes the imagery even further though: *'my most usual method is this simple attention, and such a general passionate regard to God, to whom I find myself often attached with greater sweetness and delight than that of an infant at the mother's breast: so that if I dare use the expression, I should choose to call this state the bosom of God, for the inexpressible sweetness which I taste and experience there.'*[22] What a precious thought, that we are like a baby drinking at the breast, receiving continual sustenance and strength from the very Source of life! If this seems bizarre, consider that one of the names God reveals himself with is El Shaddai, which means literally, 'the many breasted one' (Heb. *Shad*: breast). God is presenting himself to us as the All Sufficient One, the God who is More Than Enough. As both mothering and fathering are combined perfectly in the Almighty, it is entirely valid for us to see ourselves there. After all, each one of us started our human lives as a baby dependent on our mother's milk (even as the Son of God did, suckling at Mary's breast). Experts tell us that this connection is vital as we develop (with hormones, protein fats, sugars and vitamins), protecting us (transferring antibodies so we can fight off infection or illness), passing on special fatty acids (to develop brains to think, and eyes to see) and other such benefits ... we can see so many parallels in our feeding from the Lord.

This is a theme that emerges in the Scriptures, as wine and milk appear several times in Isaiah and the Song of Songs–this refers to the

---

[22] *The Practice of the Presence of God* by Brother Lawrence, 1611-1691 (Oneworld, 1993), 37-38

sustaining life-milk–such as Isaiah 55:1, *'Everyone who thirsts come to the waters; and you who have no money, come buy wine and milk without money and without cost.'* Jerusalem is pictured as a nursing mother in Isaiah 66:11, *'For you will nurse and be satisfied at her comforting breasts'* to which the Lord adds (v13), *'As a mother comforts her child, so I'll comfort you.'*

This essential sustenance of Life is what Jesus was referring to when he said, *'I tell you the truth, unless you eat the flesh of the Son of Man and drink his blood, you cannot have eternal life within you ... Anyone who eats my flesh and drinks my blood remains in me, and I in him. I live because of the Living Father who sent me; in the same way, anyone who feeds on me will live because of me.'* (John 6:53-57, excerpts) The Godhead make it plain to us, our life-source is entirely dependent upon them, yet is freely and unconditionally given to us. When we realise the love and grace given to us, then like a contented child, we can rest.

Peter makes an interesting allusion in 1 Pet 2:2-3, *'Like new-born babies, you must crave pure spiritual milk so that you will grow into a full experience of salvation. Cry out for this nourishment, now that you have had a taste of the Lord's kindness.'* Brian Simmons renders it, *'the sustaining power of God's word comes from his very breast, as it were, to nourish and strengthen our inner being ...'* (TPT) Jesus is the Word of God. The Mirror paraphrase is, *'Imagine how a new-born babe would crave nothing else but pure mother's milk; in just the same way, drink with total abandonment from the unmixed milk of the word. This is your nourishment! Once you've tasted pure grace, you are spoilt for life. Grace rules. The Lordship of Jesus is established on the dynamic of his goodness.'* In fact, one of the more amazing signs that have been seen in recent years, along with gold dust, gold teeth and scattered jewels, has been milk dripping down the walls. Signs that make you wonder!

One reason that we share the bread and wine in communion together is that we might have a reminder, a recollection, of this mystical connection, this state of being, and of our participation in the work of Christ and the Godhead. It has been called *'the Gospel in a meal'*.

Rest becomes our continuous experience as we feed on the Lord. When we take bread and wine something mystical is actually taking place. These are more than just symbols; the English word 'sacrament' has its Latin roots in the Greek word for mystery. In the Reformation people tried to reduce the communion to mere emblems, but Luther apparently fought hard for the mystical dimension to be retained. Communion is a 'common union', a participation with the Lord. St Ignatius of Antioch said it is *'the medicine of immortality, so that we should live in God through Jesus Christ.'* [23]

Taking communion should not be a religious ritual or mindless act. We do it, J.B. Torrance asserts, *'... to lift us up into a life of communion, of participation in the very triune life of God'*.[24] The background is the understanding of covenant, often lost in our Western mindsets today. When God gradually unveiled his purposes to mankind through Israel he used the Eastern tradition of a solemn covenant, which is very different, in essence, to a contract.

---

[23] Ignatius of Antioch (c. 35 – c. 107): Letter to the Ephesians, 18-20

[24] J.B. Torrance, Worship Community and the Triune God of Grace (Paternoster Press, 1996)

> *'The fallacy of legalism in all ages ... is to turn God's covenant of grace into a contract, with the most serious consequences ... In the Bible, the form of the covenant is such that the Indicatives of grace are always prior to the obligations of law and human obedience.'*[25]

God shows the depth and power of his covenant love for mankind, his *hesed* (Heb. meaning loving-kindness), to the patriarchs. Abraham, Isaac and Jacob (renamed Israel) each receive God's binding promise that he will be their all-sufficiency. A conditional covenant depended on both sides keeping to certain requirements, in which various items were exchanged, and an animal would be halved and both parties would walk between the pieces. Yet, the covenant with Abram is an unconditional covenant. After God's amazing promises to Abram–in which he says, *'All the families on earth will be blessed through you'* (Gen 12:3)–a little later in Genesis 15 this follows:

> 'God calls Abraham to slaughter the animals and birds already mentioned for a sacrifice. He doesn't tell Abram how to prepare them, but what is interesting is that Abram anticipates what God is going to do, and he butchers the livestock in the manner appropriate for a covenant ceremony, forming between the two sides of prepared meat a path of blood, such as that by which covenanters would traditionally come together. Abram keeps the sacrificed flesh untouched by the birds of prey through the day, driving them off as they look to help themselves to some fast food. As sunset

---

[25] JB Torrance *Covenant Concept*, 230, quoted by Alexandra Sophie Radcliff in *The Claim of Humanity in Christ* (Princeton, 2016), 27.

> approaches, and perhaps, as Abram is wondering what will happen next, the Lord puts his covenant partner into a deep sleep, the same kind of sleep into which the Lord sent Adam when he was separating the human being into male and female in the garden, a God-ordered sleep, in which something creative will also happen for Abram ... [the Lord then causes a smoking fire pot with a blazing torch to appear and pass between the pieces]... it is significant that the Lord put Abram into an unconscious state in order to enact this bond with him. The sleep emphasises the fact that this is not a *syntheekee* form of covenant, an agreement between two equal partners, but a *diatheekee*, a covenant in which one party makes all the moves, and the other has a passive part. The Lord is the instigator, Abram is the recipient and beneficiary of what is taking place at this moment. This emphasises the essential gift-nature of what God does for humankind.'[26]

The story actually unfolds over several chapters, as God shows quite clearly that it is by his power alone Abram/Abraham will prosper.

It is fascinating to see that this word *hesed* appears in the Hebrew translation of the Greek New Testament to render the Greek word *charis* (the familiar term for grace).

> 'This means each time an Israeli or Jewish follower of Messiah Yeshua reads their New Testament in Hebrew today, they are referencing a continuous flow of God's covenant love ... with all its richness and depth going all the way back to Genesis! ...

[26] Colin Symes, *God of Covenant, God of Grace* (Amazon, 2021), 13-14.

> a seamless garment made of the Hebrew and Greek scriptures…'[27]

Eastern covenants also involved a shared meal between the two parties (for Abraham this follows in Genesis 18), and so at the Last Supper–when Jesus is about to willingly yield his life for humanity to do its worst–and conscious that as Emmanuel through whom *'God created everything in the heavenly realms and on earth … and holds all creation together'* (extract from Colossians 1:16-17) that he, as the Lamb of God is 'dying our death', says, *'This cup is the new covenant between God and his people—an agreement confirmed with my blood, which is poured out as a sacrifice for you.'* (Luke 22:20). The word 'new' here really means 'renewed' covenant–God's *hesed* expanded for the whole of humanity. It is filial rather than judicial, in other words, is based on relationship, not on contract.

Jesus is extending to us the humble, reconciling, faithful, covenant-keeping heart of God that has been there like an unbroken thread right throughout the Old Testament (though misunderstood or sometimes obscured). He is in effect inviting us *into* his life–partaking, participating, 'feeding' on him–and says that every time we take this bread and wine, we are affirming this consistent, constant covenant that we are now one with him. *'In that day you will know that I am in my Father, I am in you and you are in me.'* (John 14:20)

The incredible revelation of the Gospel is that God, who is Spirit, who is 'Three in One', gives us not 'seven ways to be holy' or a 'philosophy of right living' as any other guru might offer, but gives us *himself*. Here is the Ancient of Days saying, 'This is my body, given for you …'

---

[27] Ibid., 27-28.

We all understand that bread is a fundamental of life, but usually we have to toil to produce it. This bread is freely given. He also gives us something tangible. The Last Supper was a Passover meal, and this bread was the *matzah* (unleavened bread), striped and pierced, broken and hidden away. Known as the *afikomen* (lit. 'hidden' or 'concealed') it foreshadowed the death, burial and resurrection of the Messiah. It echoes the manna freely provided for Israel in the desert–a daily provision that could not be hoarded for tomorrow–and also the shewbread on the altar in the tabernacle and temple (literally 'bread-of-the-face').

Jesus has announced to his hearers, 'I am the Bread of Life', and here lays out for us a meal we can all take part in. He says, *'Do this in remembrance of me'* (Luke 22:19), in other words a 'recollection' (*anamnesis* Gk.)–a memory, a reminder–a moment of mystical connection of our participation in the work of Christ and the Godhead. 'As Teresa of Avila tells her convent sisters, "all three Persons" have "so much ... mercy and kindness"that it is possible to experience this "divine company" in the "deep centre of the soul".'[28]

Memory evokes response! Have you ever caught a scent on the breeze that immediately brings back to mind somewhere you have been, or heard a sound or tune that instantly reminds you of something from childhood? The smell of woodsmoke or an orchard in bloom. The sound of a cockerel or a familiar song; for me it would be the Beatles 'Hey, Jude'! Or maybe a visual image awakens memories: a sunrise, or kicking through leaves in the autumn? Apparently, we only need to hear something for 4 minutes for it to

---

[28] Quoted by Carmen Avevido Butcher, translator, in *Practice of the Presence: A Revolutionary Translation* (Broadleaf Books, 2022).

lodge in our 'echoic memory', and positive images have proved effective in healing false memories. Jesus reminds us, *'The one who eats my body and drinks my blood lives in me, and I live in him. The Father of life sent me, and he is my life. In the same way, the one who feeds upon me, I will become his life. I am not like the bread your ancestors ate and later died. I am the living Bread that comes from heaven. Eat this Bread and you will live forever!'* (John 6:55-58 TPT) As we share in communion we are declaring, 'I am recalling the covenant benefits of Christ's vicarious work that apply to me, now and always.' This is not just a looking back but a present awareness of reality.

The cup of wine was offered at the end of the meal–understood by many to be the fourth and final cup in the Passover feast–a symbol of restoration and completeness; *'After supper he took another cup of wine and said, "This cup is the new covenant between God and his people—an agreement confirmed with my blood, which is poured out as a sacrifice for you."'* (Luke 22:20) This, Jesus said, was his blood, shed for our redemption, cutting us off at the root from our bondage to the sin-mindset. As we share in this 'eucharist' (meal of thanks) we acknowledge that we were co-crucified with Christ, and co-raised with him, to live now as New Creations in his Kingdom: one epitomised by Sabbath **rest**.

As with the counter-narrative from the start in the Garden account, so there is in life a 'false bread' and a 'false wine' that compete with this covenant meal. Wine can be a symbol of judgement or blessing, and the Passover weaves these themes together. The Book of Proverbs notes that those who do not walk the way of wisdom *'...eat the bread of wickedness and drink the wine of violence.'* (Prov 4:17 NIV) This food from the Tree of the Knowledge of Good and Evil promises a false rest, as if we have fed on junk food and it has not brought long term benefit. This, like the warnings in the letters to the Galatians or Hebrews, highlights to us how ridiculous it would be to ignore who we now are and try to find this through our own efforts or intentions!

This table *'re-presents what Christ finished on the cross'* and *'stretches beyond time and space, back to Abraham, Peter, John...and forward to our great-grandchildren'*, as through the Incarnation *'Jesus has mingled his divine nature with our earthly nature'*[29]–a mystical union in which we are healed and restored by the one who entered our broken, messy state as a human being, to redeem us from the inside. It is indeed *'the Gospel in a meal'.* It should not be a sombre affair–the early church had 'love feasts' on the first day of the week (albeit Paul had to correct a few misuses)–as we remember that it was *'for the joy set before him that Jesus endured the cross'* (Hebrews 12:2), and we are invited to fix our eyes on him and live in that joy. Rest is in one sense a by-product of our participation in Christ: **joy and rest go together**.

---

[29] John Crowder in his *Sacraments* video series, August 2022.

SIX | The Season of Singing

The Song of Songs has been understood by the church through the centuries as more than just a steamy love poem; it is an incredibly beautiful description of the passionate love the Lord has for his redeemed, his Bride.

In Songs Chapter 2 the Shepherd-King describes the girl as his darling, his 'fair one'. Brian Simmons points out that the Hebrew roots mean 'my complete one', 'my fullness.' There then follows a wonderful, lyrical passage which contrasts what is over, the winter, the dryness, the hiding, with the new season that has come as *'the rains have soaked the earth and left it bright with blossoming flowers'*, the Season of Singing, of awakening and revealing. We can see this as a picture of where we are now because of the Gospel; Jesus *is* this season.

> *The one I love calls to me:*
> *Arise, my dearest. Hurry, my darling.*
> *Come away with me!*
> *I have come as you have asked*
> *to draw you to my heart and lead you out.*
> *For now is the time, my beautiful one.*
> *The season has changed,*
> *the bondage of your barren winter has ended,*
> *and the season of hiding is over and gone.*
> *The rains have soaked the earth*
> *and left it bright with blossoming flowers.*
> *The season for singing and pruning the vines has arrived.*

I hear the cooing of doves in our land,
filling the air with songs to awaken you
and guide you forth.
Can you not discern this new day of destiny
breaking forth around you?
The early signs of my purposes and plans
are bursting forth.
The budding vines of new life
are now blooming everywhere.
The fragrance of their flowers whispers,
"There is change in the air."
(Songs 2:10-13a TPT)

Often the Charismatic church has been looking for something else that is new, something around the corner, a new season, some secret 'key', without realising the depth of the season we are actually in through Christ. Although he may continue to reveal new wonders, new dimensions in our understanding, God cannot give us more than he has given in his Son! Consider Jesus' statements: *'my fullness I give you'* and *'if you drink of me, you will never thirst again.'* He is the fullness *'that fills all in all'*, the Alpha and Omega. We are not waiting for something or someone else!

The Song of Songs anticipates the abundance of a blossoming garden through this new season, which is Jesus Christ, the promised Messiah. This vibrant garden theme in fact recurs in the Scriptures, beginning in Genesis and remerging in many prophetic and poetic passages. After the anguish in the Garden of Gethsemane, the resurrection takes place in a garden (God is even mistaken by Mary Magdalene as the gardener) and in the amazing imagery of Revelation, the culmination of all things is finally presented in a flourishing, verdant, garden setting where trees with healing leaves grow on the banks of the River of Life.

As already noted, our worship songs can all too often emphasise separation, asking Jesus to come to us, when all along he has declared that *he is in us* and there is now no distance between us. These songs have taken an Old Covenant stance where we feel we must invite the Lord to meet with us. But the Gospel teaches us that the old, separated self died with him on the cross; we are now one with him, born from above. Do we not really believe we live in him and he in us?

So often I have heard people pray from a mindset of lack. While I do not advocate seeing the world through rose-tinted spectacles, we should rather be viewing everything now through the lens of Christ. Yes, we need to be authentic and have a trusted group with whom we can be absolutely honest (hence the need for *ecclesia*), but our perspective should be as those who are *'seated in Christ in heavenly places'* (Ephesians 2:6). So therefore, our mindset and our language changes. We expect the outcome to be good.

The Old Testament prophets spoke of the Messianic Age in this way. Against the backdrop of the poor state of the nation and the growing Assyrian threat, Isaiah prophesies of this, anticipating a time when each person would live in God (and be drawn into the relational dance of the Trinity through our union with the Son). *'Each one will be like a shelter from the wind and a refuge from the storm, like streams of water in the desert and the shadow of a great rock in a thirsty land.'* (Is 32:2) This watery theme continues in the middle chapters of Isaiah: a picture of the Spirit, of favour, refreshing, abundance and the limitless supply of God in contrast to wasteland, *'Until at last the Spirit is poured out on us from heaven. Then the wilderness will become a fertile field, and the fertile field will yield bountiful crops.'* (Is 32:15) *'Water will gush forth in the wilderness and streams in the desert. The burning sand will become a pool, the thirsty ground bubbling springs.'* (Is 35:6-7) *'I will make rivers flow on barren heights, and springs within the valleys. I will turn the desert into pools of water, and the parched ground into springs.'* (Is 41:18) This is a transformation! These are opposites, because God loves to *'call things that are not as though they are.'* The result, Isaiah continues, is that, *'I will put in the desert the cedar and the acacia, the myrtle and the olive. I will set junipers in the wasteland, the fir and the cypress together.'* (Is 41:19) This points to a miraculous age–these trees would not normally grow together. In Christ, everything changes, for *'Nothing is impossible with God.'*

In another place he says, *'The LORD will guide you always; he will satisfy your needs in a sun-scorched land and will strengthen your frame. You will be like a well-watered garden, like a spring whose waters never fail.'* (Is 58:11) Do we see ourselves this way, as a well-watered garden? I sometimes hear people speak of being dry. That might be a genuine perception or a feeling, but it is not who we are now in Christ. Jesus said that we would have within us a *'spring of water welling up [literally gushing] to eternal life'* (John 4) and *'rivers of living water'* flowing from our hearts (John 7). These wonderful attributes are ours not because we've earned them through fasting or prayer or obtained enough 'Saint' points on some heavenly scale. They are ours because Jesus has fulfilled all that was necessary as the Last Adam, the perfect, spotless Lamb of God who, as an example of us, is our righteousness in God. We now live 'in Christ', adopted and accepted, sharing in his inheritance through the incredible grace extended to us.

Returning to Song of Songs Chapter 2, we catch the Lord's heart for us: we are to live now in the springtime of the Messianic age–v14 *'For you are my dove, hidden in the split-open rock'*–perhaps we can see here the side of Christ, opened by the soldier's spear. *'All mankind may enter there if they will...'* wrote Julian of Norwich.[30]

> *Arise, my love, my beautiful companion,*
> *and run with me to the higher place.*
> *For now is the time to arise and come away with me.*
> *For you are my dove, hidden in the split-open rock.*
> *It was I who took you and hid you up high*
> *in the secret stairway of the sky.*
> *Let me see your radiant face and hear your sweet voice.*
> *How beautiful your eyes of worship*
> *and lovely your voice in prayer.*
> *You must catch the troubling foxes,*
> *those sly little foxes that hinder our relationship.*
> *For they raid our budding vineyard of love*
> *to ruin what I've planted within you.*
> *Will you catch them and remove them for me?*
> *We will do it together.* (Songs 2:13b-15 TPT)

Thoughts can raid the vineyards of our minds. Fears, shame, sense of inadequacy, exclusion or hopelessness. *'You must catch the troubling foxes, those sly little foxes that hinder our relationship...we will do it together.'* (v15) The Lord's appeal to us in the Gospel is *metanoia*–think differently–see things from my perspective. Again, it comes back to our mindset, to be transformed by the renewing of our minds.

---

[30] The Tenth Revelation, Julian of Norwich, *Revelations of Divine Love.*

So we can expect, as New Creations, to live in the context of abundance. This does not mean we have to 'name it and claim it' or equate God's blessing with ostentatious wealth. Rather, it is an underlying expectation that we live from the hand of God who is Goodness itself, as well as and our Source and Strength. This can apply in a rural village in a developing country as much as in a sophisticated, complex city. It speaks primarily of our inner world, the 'Kingdom of God within' which will undoubtably affect our outer world of health, home, family, work, relationships and all manner of endeavours we undertake as participants in the Godhead.

The Springtime context of this passage speaks of new growth, of youthfulness. God may be the Ancient of Days, but he is also the youngest in the universe! There is something playful and fun about the Godhead, that is maybe surprising to some, but delightful to discover–why do you think we enjoy fun and humour anyway? When we live from rest, we find our *'youth is renewed like the eagles'* (Ps 103:5). How sad for us to 'grow up' and lose that light-hearted pleasure in life. *'Truly I tell you, unless you change and become like little children, you will never enter the kingdom of heaven ... '* (Matt 18:3) Child-like wonder and expectation are at the heart of the Kingdom.

SEVEN | Unanswerable questions

As human beings, we are all aware that life on this planet entails living with loose ends! The reality is that at times we are left perplexed by actualities and events, however much we are trusting or hopeful about the outcome. Even St Paul says, *'We are pressed on every side by troubles, but we are not crushed. We are perplexed, but not driven to despair. We are hunted down, but never abandoned by God. We get knocked down, but we are not destroyed.'* (2 Corinthians 4:8-9) Brian Simmons says this could be rendered, 'perplexed but not thoroughly perplexed', or the Aramaic can be translated, 'We are corrected but not condemned.' There is far more to our multifaceted existence than we currently understand–quantum science even shows us that–but Paul notes in the same passage that we are like common clay jars that carry a glorious treasure within, so that God will get the glory. The focus is on him. *'For God, who said, "Let there be light in the darkness," has made this light shine in our hearts so we could know the glory of God that is seen in the face ['in the face-to-face presence' TPT] of Jesus Christ. We now have this light shining in our hearts, but we ourselves are like fragile clay jars containing this great treasure. This makes it clear that our great power is from God, not from ourselves'* (2 Corinthians 4:6-7).

A lack of rest is often due to an underlying anxiety. This can be about many things–again, we are complex beings–and we cannot judge another person's feelings. Childhood trauma, chemical imbalance, medical side effects, exposure to unhealthy spiritual influences … often a subliminal sense of abandonment or orphaning is at the root. If we haven't really come to know the Truth about our being, then we will not experience the freedom that he brings. The Scriptures say that *metanoia* is required: thinking differently, seeing things from God's perspective. This has traditionally been translated 'repentance' in English, which unfortunately suggests 'penance' and handwringing introspection, but is in fact a much more positive action. A renewed mind sees the events of our lives through God's eyes.

Knowing that we are fully known and loved–and that this was from the very start (before we had any thought of responding, for or against)–leads to great assurance. God loves us and he hasn't changed his mind about us! It has been discovered that our early years, even from the womb, can have a profound impact on our adult lives. Childhood trauma, or abuse during our earlier life, can rob us of a sense of self-worth and peace and trigger all sorts of responses. Skilled counselling may be very helpful here, but fundamentally lasting change comes when we know that our old self died mystically with Christ on the cross, and that our new self (our True Self, as sometimes referred to) is one with him, made clean, sustained by his life. He hung naked on the cross to bear every sense of shame we carried, he voluntarily drank the very worst of mankind's wrongdoing 'to the dregs', accepting the cruellest, unfairest venom and torture we could possibly inflict.

This was not, as has sadly been taught, the Father punishing the Son, for where would the other members of the Trinity be but also in Christ? Something of the mystery is here. *'For God was in Christ reconciling the world to himself...'* (2 Cor 5:19) Paul writes. Rather it was the Godhead identifying with our extreme pain and sense of isolation *('My God, my God, why have you forsaken me...'* quoting Psalm 22). It is a more recent notion that the Father would turn his back on the Son–not the view of the early church fathers–but as that

Psalm 22 goes on to say, *'he has not abandoned his beloved'*. Jesus himself states that the Father never leaves him. This was not God punishing Christ for us–Isaiah 53 notes that this was our idea, verse 4: *'we thought that his troubles were a punishment from God'*–but rather, the most humble, loving act of our Creator God who submitted himself to our very worst act of all time, in order that he might heal mankind, once and for all, of the curse of Adam's fall.

I can remember experiencing something of God's presence and guidance from early childhood, while belonging with my parents to a traditional, more institutional church. Becoming exposed to a more evangelical, charismatic environment in my mid-teens was at first very exciting and real. However, I soon took on a whole series of demands, reading many of the paperbacks that were passed my way. Before long I was thinking, have I prayed enough? have I fasted enough? am I a serious Christian or just a 'chocolate soldier' (as one writer put it)? Then I was concerned about whether I was really doing God's will ... or would I be one to whom the Lord would eventually say, 'I never knew you'?

I had gained a place at one of Britain's oldest universities, but I got myself (and my poor parents) into quite a state over whether I should go or not. My memory of that summer is that all the peace and joy I'd experienced in finding a more authentic faith had evaporated, only to be replaced by stress (and fear of God's displeasure). Thankfully, others more mature than me encouraged me that I should still go to Edinburgh and study architecture, my chosen subject, and I'm glad to say, 'the rest is history'. I can now see how God wove his purposes through the warp and weft of my life; despite a few more ups and downs, I found where I belonged. He has continued to reveal himself to me faithfully over the decades.

The way we approach the Scriptures can have a bearing on our sense of rest. While we treasure the revelation held there, we have at times had an unhealthy view of the Holy Bible, almost raising it to be one of the Trinity (Father, Son and Holy Bible) or forming a 'quad-rinity'. Yet in so doing, we created issues we were never intended to have; the Scriptures were God-breathed accounts to give us a faithful, reliable witness of the Word, who is Jesus Christ, and convey to us the Gospel. Jesus made it clear: *'You search the Scriptures because you think they give you eternal life. But the Scriptures point to me!'* (John 5:39)

God in his wisdom chose to do this through the lives and writings of countless men and women, passed down and recorded through the centuries. We often put these Old Testament people on a pedestal and teach their stories as codes of behaviour for us to follow, without realising that they were all the time pointing towards God's ultimate revelation in his Son. *'Long ago God spoke many times and in many ways to our ancestors through the prophets. And now in these final days, he has spoken to us through his Son.'* (Hebrews 1:1-2a) *'...He is the sum total of every utterance of God. He is who the Prophets pointed to and we are his immediate audience.'* (extract from verse 1 in the Mirror)

Jesus had to explain this to the two disciples he joined on the road to Emmaus, after the resurrection. He showed them how the Scriptures pointed to him!

Similarly, we can read some passages and become confused by the language used, or the seeming strictness of the message. However, we need to learn to see all of scripture though the lens of Christ, in whom we now exist. God is not changeable in the way that we can be, he does not have two faces (like the Roman god Janus, a man with two heads who could be both kind and mean). If we want to know what he is like, we just need to look at Jesus, for as Jesus explained to Philip, *'If you've seen me, you've seen the Father'*. (John 14:9)

While our focus rightly is on the Lord–as Paul says, *'For everything comes from him and exists by his power and is intended for his glory. All glory to him forever! Amen'* (Rom 11:36)–the wonderful truth is that his focus is on us! We are the object of his love! So, when we read the parables or sayings of Jesus, which sometimes contain stern warnings, we need to understand what he was doing. He was addressing an inadequate D.I.Y. religious system and a mindset that 'loved darkness rather than light' and exposing its total redundancy in the light of the love of God. When we read of wise and foolish virgins, we need to realise that we are not one of them; we are the Bride at the wedding.[31] When we read of sheep and goats being separated, we need to remember that we are not living on a knife edge, in danger of being rejected, we are now in Christ. This was describing the Father's desire that only what is good may exist in his kingdom. Any world systems that deny that will indeed disappear. When we understand that the nature of God's judgement is not punitive but restorative, we do not fear the Day of Judgement. Paul Young refers to the insights of the nineteenth century Scottish author George Macdonald, who said that if we really understood the nature of God's love we would just run to him with open arms and say, 'judge me to the core and burn out of me everything that keeps me from being fully human and fully alive!'[32] In fact, Jesus said that the devil was judged at the cross (Jn 12:31, 16:11); we now live on the other side of the cross.

---

[31] Bill Vanderbush made this point of all the parables, speaking in Edinburgh, 2018.
[32] Wm. Paul Young https://inaspaciousplace.wordpress.com/2017/05/07/william-paul-young-trinity-the-soul-of-creation-12d/

Sometimes our distorted theology can cause unrest. At the root of this is often a fear of punishment. What should we understand about hell? Many scholars have delved into this, but the Medieval pictures of eternal torture chambers are based on a misunderstanding. In fact, there are four different words often translated 'hell' in our New Testaments, and each had a specific meaning in the first century. [33] God's clear desire is that 'none should perish'. So, what are these descriptions of fire referring to? Perhaps the fire of his love is so intense that, as Wm. Paul Young says, *'it burns up anything that is not of love's kind'*. Of course, we are free to reject his love–that will certainly feel like fire in the face of the purest love–but he will never stop loving us. The Apostle Paul certainly teaches that the wood, hay and stubble do not survive; it is the treasure of the Kingdom, the revelation of Jesus in us, that continues in eternity. Brad Jersak notes that amazingly the gates of the eternal city in Revelation are always open–and the invitation remains, 'Come!' None of us fully know what this all means; what we do know is that the love of the Father is dependable. *'The Father himself loves you,'* Jesus reassures the disciples.

The esteemed Scottish theologians T.F. and J.B. Torrance studied under Karl Barth and drew much on the teaching of the early Church Fathers, including Irenaeus, Origen and Athanasius. In her excellent book Alexandra Radcliffe noted T.F. Torrance's view that 'God does not send the damned to hell, nor did he create the hell they experience; God loves the whole of humanity everlastingly'. It is in rejecting this love that one can experience a hell of one's own creation: 'To choose finally and forever–unfathomable mystery of

[33] Sheol, Hades, Gehenna and Tartarus. Brad Jersak cast light on these and Hope, Hell and the New Jerusalem, in his excellent book *Her Gates Will Never Be Shut* (WIPF and STOCK Publishers, 2009).

iniquity–to say "No" to Jesus is to be held in a hell of one's own choosing and making. It is not God who makes hell, for hell is a contradiction of all that is of God.' The Torrances (both T.F. and J.B.) argued that the work of Christ was a very real and total judgement on humanity's sin and guilt, but equally a positive act of full reconciliation of man, through the blood of Jesus. 'The Torrances believe that this acceptance of humanity is irrevocable: "To reverse it would be to bring Christ back to the cross again, and to deny the reality of what he has already done."'[34]

> For the first five centuries of the church, the predominant view of the final judgment was not retributive, but restorative. Most of the early fathers believed in the ultimate restoration of all things (apokatastasis), that Christ's finished work would ultimately be a cosmic success. It was not until the sixth century when Emperor Justinian (not a bishop) called a church council and took it upon himself to anathematize certain readings of Origen (without a vote of the clergy), that this mainstream hopeful perspective of the "end things" got supplanted by another more dismal view. Justinian, who expanded the empire by blood, sword and oppression, preferred the minority view of Augustine: that of an eternal conscious torment version of retributive, unending hell for the reprobates. Church and empire could not be motivated by the love of Christ alone. People would grow slothful and disobedient unless they feared a God who literally tortured people forever. Augustine's minority view of the afterlife (he couldn't even read scriptures in Greek) shifted to the

[34] T.F. Torrance *Atonement*, 156, quoted by Alexandra Sophie Radcliff, *The Claim of Humanity in Christ* (Princeton, 2016).

> mainstream, an ominous doctrine endorsed by the emperor to build "Christendom" and expand the empire by crippling, eternal threat. To this day, most folks think this is the only way to view Jesus' judgment parables, despite centuries of better, earlier perspectives.[35]

We are not made for fear of punishment; *'Perfect love cast out fear'*. (1 John 4:18) We are made to share in the life of the Godhead. 'In the Torrances' scheme of salvation, our works by the Spirit are the fruit of participating in Christ. Rather than being turned in upon ourselves, worrying about whether we are bearing enough fruit for final justification, J.B. encourages the believer to fix their eyes upon Jesus. Christ has lived a life of perfect obedience in our place, taking full judgement upon himself and securing our acceptance, so that as we participate in him in freedom and joy, we might bear the fruit of the Spirit.'[36] When we really receive this in our heart, it can inform our head and we can live from true rest.

Living content with loose ends implies trust in the Lord. The need to tie up all loose ends comes from our desire to control and is in fact a fruit of the Tree of the Knowledge of Good and Evil. Instead, living 'present' in I AM, living from the River, living from the sustaining Source, is feeding from the Tree of Life: ultimately Jesus.

---

[35] John Crowder, commenting online 2023.

[36] Alexandra Sophie Radcliff, *The Claim of Humanity in Christ* (Princeton, 2016), 104.

EIGHT | Harmony and rhythm

Rest does not necessarily equate with inactivity. In fact, rest can imply movement, but a movement in harmony with heaven. There is a 'sweet spot' in which activity flows from rest, in the same way that Jesus could say, *'My Father is always working, and so am I.'* (John 5:17)

I have never felt that I have a particular gift for drumming. Yet, in a drum circle, each player may have a simple part. When our friend Martin Neil[37] has led a drum workshop in Wellsprings, I have been amazed how my humble, repeated 'dum-tat-tat' on a djembe will weave into a wonderful pattern, as Martin leads us in a West African or Samoan rhythm that contains a distinct, enthralling pulse. This reflects the rhythm that exists in the whole of Creation, which we are told is formed of waves of energy, every quantum particle vibrating in harmony with the universe. Perhaps rest is an environment in which all that the Godhead has spoken into being can thrive together, a healthy symbiosis in which mankind can enjoy the fullness of life we were made for.

I may not be gifted in percussion, but I have already mentioned my love of sailing. There is more to that than just hoisting sails; when the sails are properly trimmed, they form the perfect curved shape that propels the yacht forward. When heading into the wind, the air travelling around the outside of the sail has to move faster, so the

---

[37] Martin & Rebekah Neil have a passion for releasing indigenous rhythms, see www.voicesfromthenations.org

pressure drops, and the boat heels and is effectively 'pulled' forward. When the large sail (a jib or genoa) at the bows is correctly set, the tell-tales (coloured marker threads) lie flat and horizontal, and one can actually sense the boat 'lift' as it finds this sweet spot. A skilled helmsman will learn the feel of a boat and respond to the vagaries of the wind to remain in this symbiotic alignment. No work from strenuous rowing or a noisy outboard motor is required; it is another form of rest.

My two sisters-in-law can both be described as having 'green fingers'; they have a gift for growing plants and have created gorgeous, productive gardens. In fact, the whole sphere of cultivation is something deep in our DNA that goes back to the very beginning, in which we are made in the image of One who planted a garden. *'Then the LORD God planted a garden in Eden in the east, and there he placed the man he had made. The LORD God made all sorts of trees grow up from the ground—trees that were beautiful and that produced delicious fruit.'* (Genesis 2:8-9a) In the Genesis story mankind was asked to tend and care for this garden and enjoy the bountiful fruit it produced–a relationship of trust in the goodness of God.

We can see in the nature of the planet how nothing is wasted, again it is a symbiotic cycle of life in which everything returns to the soil and then new life emerges. Sadly, the lie that emerged from the eating of the forbidden tree has led to a break from this harmony; mankind has dominated and exploited the planet, raping the natural resources for selfish or short-term gain. Industrialisation and mechanisation have led to much being wasted: once something has ceased to be useful it is usually thrown away. Modern farming methods have often overworked the land, so that it has to be controlled by chemicals and replenished with artificial fertilisers. A UN report stated that 'generating three centimetres of topsoil takes 1,000 years, and if current rates of degradation continue all of the world's topsoil could be gone within 60 years.' [38] This has been disputed by some, but 'research suggests ... a fall in soil quality in the long term with continuous farming. Increasingly it is thought that, for food production to be sustainable in the long term, we need to adjust agricultural techniques. For example, one possible approach is called Conservation Agriculture, which includes reduced tillage, permanent ground cover including cover crops to protect soil structure, and crop rotation.' [39] Many are doing exciting research into these things. People who have experimented with organic methods or allowed for 're-wilding' have noted how nature has a way of finding a healthy balance, keeping pests or disease in check, and flourishing again. Perhaps we need to learn again what it is for the land to be truly at rest.

There must also be a 'sweet spot' in harmony between humans in which kindness in our relationships, an environment of rest and an atmosphere of shared delight are to the fore (in other words, the Kingdom of God as in *'righteousness, peace and joy'* Romans 14:17b). Jesus came as the Prince of Peace heralded with *'Peace on earth and goodwill towards men'*, and after the resurrection, he announced 'Peace' to those listening. We were made for community because the Godhead is a 'sweet community'. This is why, in an individualistic, broken society, we should cherish every healthy expression of coming together in mutual care and support. The *ecclesia* (the church or 'gathered assembly') was brought into being as a prophetic

---

[38] Article in Scientific American, 5 December 2014.
[39] UK fact checking resource, www.whatthesciencesays.org, 20 December 2019.

demonstration of this loving, interdependent family. As noted, Francois du Toit explains that the Greek word *ecclesia* derives from **ek**, a preposition denoting origin, and **klesia** from **kaleo**, to surname, thus referring to our original identity. The church is where we come together to remind one another of who we really are.

While I believe we have to be intentional about creating community in the complex world we live in, nevertheless it will thrive when we allow it to be sustained by the Finished Work of the Cross. Here we see that there is no distance between us or the Lord, and no divisions or hierarchy due to race, gender or wealth.

'The life of grace is not an effort on our part to achieve a goal we set ourselves. It is a continually renewed attempt simply to believe that someone else has done all the achieving that is needed and to live in relationship with that person, whether we achieve or not. If that doesn't seem like much to you, you're right: it isn't. And, as a matter of fact, the life of grace is even less than that. It's not even our life at all, but the life of that Someone Else rising like a tide in the ruins of our death.' (Robert Farrar Capon)[40]

Over the past century or so, there has been much exploration of the field of quantum mechanics. Here this sense of harmony and rhythm has been found to exist in the universe, from the mega scale of over 200 billion galaxies to the micro scale of the smallest particle. As noted, everything is formed from waves of energy. There is a mysterious effect called 'quantum entanglement' in which two subatomic particles, such as a pair of photons or electrons, may be

---

[40] Robert Farrar Capon, *Between Noon & Three: Romance, Law & the Outrage of Grace* (Wm. B. Eerdmans, 1997).

linked together, even if separated by vast distances. A change induced in one will mysteriously also appear in the other. Other bizarre phenomena have been detected, in which matter only exists once it is observed. This prompts a rethink about the scientific cause-and-effect approach we have been schooled in over recent generations, and offers a glimpse into a world we cannot explain: the realm of prayer, miracles, signs and wonders.

Isaiah 40:31 is a familiar verse about waiting on the Lord, *'they who wait for the LORD shall renew their strength; they shall mount up with wings like eagles; they shall run and not be weary; they shall walk and not faint.'* (ESV) It has been pointed out that the word we often translate 'wait' (Heb. *kawa*) also means 'entwine' or 'entangle'– someone commented, 'Imagine two ropes being braided into each other, so that in the end, you don't know where one starts and the other one ends'–so while Isaiah's prophecy suggests renewal through peaceful rest, it also implies union with the Lord. Again, Godfrey Birtill has captured this vibrantly in a song:

> I entangle into you
> Your life is my life
> Your strength is my strength
> Your health is my health
> I entangle into you
> I entangle into you
>
> Your Love is my love
> Your Joy is my joy
> Your Peace is my peace
> I entangle into you

They that wait upon the Lord
Shall run and not grow weary
They that wait upon the Lord
Shall walk and not faint
They that wait upon the Lord
Shall rise up like an eagle
On thermals of grace, soaring on grace.

I entangle into you
When you died, I died
When you rose, I rose
Where you are, I am
Entangled into you

Wrapped in you I live, wrapped in you I move
Wrapped in you I have my being, length of days.[41]

This captures the sense of rest that we found in leaning back into the amazing love of the Lord, aware of our union in Christ. It furthermore spurs us on to consider who we are now, not in a triumphalist sense but in humble wonder at the work of the Lord. The scripture says we are being *'transformed from glory to glory'* (2 Corinthians 3:18) and the word used for transformation is the same word used of Jesus being 'transfigured' on the mountain: *'But all of us who are Christians have no veils on our faces, but reflect like mirrors the glory of the Lord. We are transfigured by the Spirit of the Lord in ever-increasing splendour into his own image.'* (Phillips) The Message paraphrases that passage this way:

---

[41] Godfrey Birtill & Justin Paul Abraham, 2018 ©Whitefield Music UK (Album: *Entangled & Intrinsically Linked*, 2019).

Whenever, though, they turn to face God as Moses did, God removes the veil and there they are—face-to-face! They suddenly recognize that God is a living, personal presence, not a piece of chiselled stone. And when God is personally present, a living Spirit, that old, constricting legislation is recognized as obsolete. We're free of it! All of us! Nothing between us and God, our faces shining with the brightness of his face. And so we are transfigured much like the Messiah, our lives gradually becoming brighter and more beautiful as God enters our lives and we become like him.

This gives us confidence as we pray, for we don't have to work up something. John G. Lake said, 'I am a believer in the partnership of man and God. There is a fusing, a symphonising of God and man; the two become one. Not a saved man and a glorious God. But man fused into God and God fused into man, one divine creation. When Moses stood at the Red Sea, it was not Moses and God; it was just God. We say: 'Lord, make me a channel' leaving ourselves separated from God in our thought and expecting God to pour his spiritual power and blessing through us. That is not the highest thing. There is a greater experience than that in God's word: it is where you and God are one. Your whole body, your whole soul, your whole mind, your whole heart, your whole spirit begins to move in the rhythm and fusion and symphony of the eternal God; one in heart, one in mind, you and God as one. Moses tried to back out of this relationship. God told him to shut up and stop praying and get on with the job! '...You stretch out your hand over the sea and you divide it!'[42]

[42] John Graham Lake was a Canadian-American leader in the Pentecostal movement that began in the early 20th century, and is known as a faith healer, missionary, and with Thomas Hezmalhalch, co-founder of the Apostolic Faith Mission of South Africa.

This does not imply that we are God–we are still distinct as his creation–but that there is a 'mystical union'. This is the dimension that Paul refers to in Romans 8 when he speaks of *'all creation groaning'* as it waits for the sons of God to arise. The empowering flows from this state of rest.

NINE | By still waters

We cannot consider rest without reference to what is probably everyone's favourite psalm, Psalm 23. It is no accident that this follows Psalm 22 in the psalter–the most quoted Messianic psalm, that Jesus declares from on the cross–and before Psalm 24–one that celebrates the Lord as Creator of all (and could be said to foreshadow the Apostles Creed in this regard). Psalm 23 is often read or sung at funerals, with the sense of R.I.P., 'Rest in Peace'... yet it is really a celebration of the God in whom we walk through *life*, dwelling in his rest amid the ups and downs of earthly existence.

The Passion translation of Psalm 23 is refreshing in its interpretation of well-known words. It is the testimony of a pastoralist, David, the shepherd boy who would later become king.

> *Yahweh is my best friend and my shepherd.*
> *I always have more than enough.*
> *He offers a resting place for me in his luxurious love.*
> *His tracks take me to an oasis of peace near the quiet brook of bliss.*
> *That's where he restores and revives my life.*
> *He opens before me the right path*
> *and leads me along in his footsteps of righteousness*
> *so that I can bring honour to his name.*

Brian Simmons notes that friend and shepherd are interchangeable in the Hebrew, and that a shepherd knows instinctively where the sheep are going to be well fed, resting in safety.[43] The sense of 'still waters' in verse two can speak to us on many levels ... an oasis that never runs dry and a place where we know the bliss of encounter with the Lord. *'What bliss you experience when your heart is pure! For then your eyes will open to see more and more of God.'* (Matt 5:8 TPT) Our hearts are pure not through self-effort, but by recognising our innocence in Christ, thereby understanding more and more of who we really are and who he really is. The Hebrew speaks here of *'the waters of a resting place'*.[44]

I love the way Francois du Toit interprets this: *'by the waters of reflection my soul remembers who I am.'* The preceding psalm says, *'All the ends of the earth shall remember and return to the Lord'* (Ps 22:27 ESV)–the Father, Son and Spirit lead us to a place where we can discover again our true identity which has always been wrapped up in who they are, as we were made by them in the image of God. In mirror-like waters we see reflected the face of Christ, who is now our life in God.

The beauty of Psalm 23 is that it embraces the whole of life, acknowledging that there are times that are hard as well as those that are easy:

> *Even when your path takes me through*
> *the valley of deepest darkness,*
> *fear will never conquer me, for you already have!*
> *Your authority is my strength and my peace.*

---

[43] Simmons notes in the Passion Translation that the Greek word 'to love' is *agapao*, merging the word *ago* 'to lead like a shepherd' with *pao* 'to rest'. There is something profound here about resting in God's love.
[44] Ibid., *menuha* (Heb).

The comfort of your love takes away my fear.
I'll never be lonely, for you are near.

This is often rendered 'the valley of the shadow of death'. If rest finds its source in the Person of Jesus Christ, then it does not depend on external circumstances. Our mortality and the complexities of human life are aspects of our humanity that 'our best friend' has fully identified with, entering into our suffering even to the point of physical death, in order that we might instead share his life, indeed, feed from the Tree of Life throughout our earthly existence. If you are suffering today, he does not stand apart from you, looking on ... he is there, suffering with you, as you dwell in him and he dwells in you in perfect union.

You become my delicious feast
even when my enemies dare to fight.
You anoint me with the fragrance of your Holy Spirit;
you give me all I can drink of you until my cup overflows.

With resonances of the Communion meal, we are reminded that Christ is our food, our feast, our very sustenance. *'Unless you eat the flesh and drink the blood of the Son of Man, you have no life in you.'* (John 5:53 ESV) There is something of mystery here, that speaks of our eternal existence being fed and nourished by the one through whom everything was created and continues to be. We have the Trinitarian life here, as oil represents the Holy Spirit, our anointing. The fragrant oils used in the temple would linger in the air, and as we rest in the empowering Spirit of God, so a sweet aroma surrounds our lives. We can recognise this in every place we see the Godhead at work today.

An overflowing cup also *'brims with blessing'* (Message) like the finest wine. The Vulgate apparently rendered this *'my chalice that inebriates me, how goodly that is'*. [45] There is a holy inebriation that accompanies the fulness of the Spirit that we can all experience. It is not earned through our efforts, rather it is discovered within us as we explore the wonders of who we are now in Christ. After all, he gave us his fulness, and the experience of history (as on the day of Pentecost) is that we are *already* 'drunk' as we enjoy the new wine! John Crowder writes, 'I believe I am already in the House of Wine, thanks to Christ's work. I rely on his efforts, not my own. If I don't feel anything, that's irrelevant. When I relax and trust that I'm fully tanked, I begin to enjoy the drink. Feeling follows faith. His work is the substance and source from which I am drinking.'[46] It is this perspective of resting in Jesus Christ that alters our walk with him. The many Christian mystics through the ages testified to this ecstatic experience as they pondered the implications of our transformation through his vicarious work.

> *So why would I fear the future?*
> *Only goodness and tender love pursue me*
> *All the days of my life.*
> *Then afterward, when my life is through,*
> *I'll return to your glorious presence to be forever with you!*

The psalm ends with this magnificent affirmation of hope, both now and eternally in the presence of God. Note how none of the benefits are contingent on the subject in the psalm, the 'sheep'–all are due to the provision and care of the Shepherd.

---

[45] Ibid., Psalm 23.

[46] John Crowder, *Mystical Union* (Sons of Thunder Publications 2010), 132.

Jesus Christ, who is God incarnate, declares to the listening crowds, *'I am the Good Shepherd'*. Now 'from the other side of the cross' we see that he has done all that is necessary for us to dwell in the green pastures, the *'resting place ... in his luxurious love'.* We do not make it happen by our belief, our repentance or our obedience; he has accomplished all this without our help! We instead awaken to the wonder of his redeeming work, made through his faith, his obedience, his love–our belief and response is really us being roused from slumber, or, to put it another way, enlightened from a darkened mindset, reminded of who we truly are. What a thrill to discover that the Godhead has been *for* us all along and made full and complete provision in the Son! He then empowers this response in our hearts, that is like an overflowing fountain or river. How often those images accompany pictures of rest!

TEN | The insouciant believer

It would be so easy to misunderstand this message about rest! Yet it is all about the Source; the outcome will probably look different for each of us, as we are unique example of his workmanship, his *poiema* (Gk.).

> As He dreamed by dawn-light,
> He wrought us from the wonder-rhyme,
> Friends to laugh with, children to nurture,
> Co-workers sharing in the Plan.
> So, breath by breath, with
> Each spoken stanza He formed this fiery imprint
> Struck from iron hard clay, yet
> Woven with silken strands of Love
> And placed in un-assailable Grace.
> Pre-empting and providing
> That the eternal anthology of man
> Might be enjoyed
> In the full light of day.[47]

We were made for this abundant life, for community, for inner freedom and rest. So often when people become converted and describe themselves as believers, their nascent delight and joy gets quickly tempered by the 'manufacturing processes' of institutional Christianity, and what was organic, free and full of life gets squeezed though a mould of performance and expectation.

---

[47] *The Poet* by David Hewitt 2013.

God however is not interested in outward appearances per se, or in the veneer of spirituality often applied through religious mindsets. He is interested rather in us discovering our life in in him, and he in us, and our participation in this blissful relationship (otherwise termed the Kingdom of God). He is in us in the warp and weft of our daily lives; he does not get shocked by anything; he is never disappointed with us or disillusioned when we trip up. 'Jesus is in you—not the Sunday morning version of you, but the broken you, the real you as you are.' [48]

Yet like children dressed initially in school clothes too big for us, we grow (or mature) to fill out who we really are now. God reveals his glory in us. Of course, as we *'put on Christ' (Rom 13:14, Eph 3:27)* we naturally cooperate; David Torrance noted how the Greek verb here uses the middle voice, and as with helping a child into a coat, implies a participation, a cooperation of the recipient.[49] Have you ever tried putting a coat onto an uncooperative child?! Yet the provision, the work, is all of the parent. David notes how we often start the wrong way with God, from guilt approaching the cross. But God starts with love and embraces us (dealing with the issue of sin as the final part, as in Leviticus, 'outside the camp'). He notes that the first covenants were nothing to do with sin. There may be a legal aspect in which we can declare to the enemy that he has no hold on us, but this is not a transaction to satisfy a reluctant God. This is a loving Father who has announced our adoption from the outset.

Ten years ago, when studying for their PhDs in Scotland, Alexandra Radcliff and her husband Jason joined in our community, and they

---

[48] Dr. Baxter Kruger at a recent conference, *Finding Home*, 2023 (Edinburgh).
[49] David Torrance, in a conversation in 2018. David was a nephew of T.F. and J.B. Torrance.

spoke at one of our gatherings. She noted how Christian faith has often been taught as us working our way up a mountain into God's presence. Then on a whiteboard she drew a picture of us sitting behind Jesus on a wooden sled, laughing with hands in the air and crying 'WHEEEEEE….!' as we sped with him down a snowy slope. 'The Christian Gospel,' she said, 'is 'WHEEEEEE….!'' This illustrates so beautifully the simple truth of our inclusion in Jesus' healing, redeeming work.

It was often the *metanoia*, the 'thinking again from a different perspective', that led the Christian mystics through the ages to times of ecstasy, as they meditated on what Christ had done. We are all unique and may find some ways more helpful than others, but making space for contemplation and meditation is of proven benefit. James Finlay writes, 'Through our renewed fidelity to our contemplative practices we learn to discern and take steps to correct any tendencies to drag around dust-gathering trophies of things past …. Sitting silent and still in meditation, walking with attentive gratitude at sunset, reaching out to cup the beloved's face in our hands, we find ourselves once again at the never-ending origins of the one unending present moment in which our lives unfold.'[50]

Living 'present' frees us from what Wm. Paul Young describes as 'future-tripping' or living in the regret for things past. Jesus gave seven famous 'I AM' statements in John's Gospel[51] and declared to the enraged, hyper-religious Pharisees that *'before Abraham was*

---

[50] James Finley, *The Contemplative Heart* (Notre Dame, IN: Sorin Books, 2000), 207.
[51] The 'I am' statements found in the Gospel of John are the bread of life (6:35), the light of the world (8:12), the door (10:7), the good shepherd (10:11, 14), the resurrection and the life (11:25), the way, the truth and the life (14:6) and the true vine (15:1).

born, I am' (John 8:56-59), making a direct link to God's self-revelation in Exodus 3. They understood clearly what he was saying: I am God incarnate. While there is nothing wrong in planning ahead or having a budget, the emphasis comes back to where we find our source, our strength, our place of rest. He wants to be the environment our lives thrive in, day by day, as with simple trust we participate in the life of the Godhead. Worry robs us of peace, affects our health, our families, our wellbeing .... We were not made for that!

Life is sometimes quite messy, but God is very much with us in the contradictions, the questions, the loose ends ... even the Apostle Paul admitted that at times he was perplexed (2 Cor 4:8) as he travelled preaching Christ to the world of his day. He reminds his readers that, formed from clay, we are like fragile clay jars. Yet the emphasis is not on the frailty, but on the glory contained within:

We now have this light shining in our hearts, but we ourselves are like fragile clay jars containing this great treasure. This makes it clear that our great power is from God, not from ourselves (2 Cor 4:7).

And now, in the glow of this glorious light and with unveiled faces we discover this treasure where it was hidden all along, in these frail skin-suits made of clay. We did not invent ourselves; we are God's idea to begin with and the dynamic of his doing and amazing engineering (2 Cor 4:7 MIR).

We have been placed in a vast garden to explore–a safe place. It's as if there is a rock garden, an arboretum, there are herbaceous plants for scent and colourful beauty, plants for food, pools, waterfalls, dramatic escarpments, wide open spaces...

Julian of Norwich was a late 14th-century English mystic who had remarkable insights into the nature of the Trinity, and the love of God. Julian became an anchorite–a medieval role in which a woman would devote her life to contemplation and prayer, enclosed in a cell or rooms adjoining a church building. There, over the next twenty years she meditated on the visions she had received and gained a beautiful revelation of the goodness of God. Our ultimate rest is closely woven with our understanding of the goodness of the Father, Son and Holy Spirit.

At a time when the church was often preaching about a distant, punitive God angry at mankind and threatening hellfire, she brought a different perspective: 'For I saw no wrath except on man's side, and he forgives that in us, for wrath is nothing but a perversity and an opposition to peace and to love.'[52] She had received a series of visions when almost at the point of death, during a time of illness in her 30th year. These surrounded the crucifixion of Christ and were notable for their intimate, visceral portrayal: '... the blood flowed hot, like a river of life, the spear wound in the Lord's side was an open void and the pericardial fluid poured out as water and blood.'

She saw motherhood there, and the depth of love in the Godhead. In the open wounds of Christ she saw a 'resting place for humanity'– true rest in his completed work. As Brother Lawrence was later to see, Julian describes how we receive our essential nurture and sustenance through the broken body of the Lord:

---

[52] Beer, Frances, ed. (1998), *Revelations of Divine Love*, translated from British Library Additional MS 37790: the Motherhood of God: an excerpt, translated from British Library MS Sloane 2477, (Rochester, New York: D.S. Brewer).

'The human mother can suckle the child with her milk. But our beloved Mother Jesus can feed us with himself. This is what he does when he tenderly and graciously offers us the blessed sacrament, which is the precious food of true life. In mercy and grace he sustains us with all the sweet sacraments. This is what he meant when he said that he was the one that holy church preaches and teaches us. In other words, Christ the Mother is entwined with the wholeness of life which includes all the sacraments, all the virtues, all the virtues of the word-made-flesh, all the goodness that holy church ordains for our benefit. The human mother can tenderly lay the child on her breast, but our tender Mother Jesus can lead us directly into his own tender breast through his sweet broken-open side. Here, he reveals a glimpse of the godhead and some of the joys of paradise with the implicit promise of eternal bliss.'[53]

Julian saw that we understand rest fully when we forget ourselves and embrace our union with Christ. When we are worried and bothered by the superficial trifles of the world-system, with its glitz and glamour, we can get self-absorbed in its shallow promises for the false self: 'For this is the cause why we be not all in ease of heart and soul: that we seek here rest in those things that are so little, wherein is no rest, and know not our God that is All-mighty, All-wise, All-good. For He is the Very Rest. God willeth to be known, and it pleaseth Him that we rest in Him; for all that is beneath Him sufficeth not us. And this is the cause why that no soul is rested till it is made nought as to all things that are made. When it is willingly made nought, for love, to have Him that is all, then is it able to receive spiritual rest.' [54]

[53] Julian of Norwich, *Revelations of Divine Love* (Long text, Ch. 60).
[54] Ibid. (Long text, Ch. 5).

Although rest is not achieved as a 'work' we do, the laying down, yielding and forgetting of our self is clearly an aspect of the grace-life, for the narcissistic, self-centred person will struggle, as they will always be trying to make things right through their own efforts. The Apostle Paul says, in the context of discussing the immorality of the day, *'You do not belong to yourself, for God bought you with a high price'* (1 Cor 6:19b-20a). This sense of us having been purchased and being God's possession, in a positive sense, is a recurring theme.

Ultimately though, Julian's message was one of hope, a deep reassurance in the abiding love of a good God: 'But all will be well, and all will be well, and all manner of things will be well.' [55]When this resonates through our being, sourced in our understanding of the incarnation and the cross, we know that whatever happens, we can rest.

Returning to the origins of 'sabbath' in the scriptures, we see the way Israel was instructed when wandering in the desert. God showed his goodness and love to them by providing the manna, a heavenly bread that was a foreshadow of Christ, the Bread of Life. They were told to gather just what they needed for each day–interestingly, it would not keep for another day, it was 'daily bread'–yet before the Sabbath day God would provide double so that they could rest. It was to follow the pattern of God resting on the Seventh Day. This was to be treated holistically; it was to be a day when animals and refugees/foreigners could rest too.

As time went on, the day was developed into a Sabbath Year (Leviticus 15) in which every seven years sufficient would be provided

---

[55] Ibid. (Long text, Ch. 27).

in seed, fruit, general provision so that the whole year would be one of rest. The land could lie fallow and replenish itself. This was a powerful picture of rest linked to trust in God. This has been shown to be a vital ingredient of a healthy lifestyle, agriculturally, physically, emotionally, even spiritually.

If that was not remarkable enough, God then told them to have a Sabbath of Sabbath years ... so after 49 years there would be a year of Jubilee. At this seminal time there would not only be provision for the year, but slaves were to be released, property returned, the people would live in exceptional blessing. God had faith that his people would live from his goodness ... the year of the favour of the Lord. These pictures speak to us of how he has always been the sustainer and provider for all we need in life: the Trinity invite us to find our security in their faithful love.

Did the Children of Israel ever enter into this heavenly economy? We are not told. Yet the Lord is clearly laying out a pattern based around trust and rest ... the two areas we often struggle with. We may not be expected to take this format literally today, but the understanding that our lives are completely dependent on the Godhead remains true. Jesus tells us not to worry about the practicalities of life–what we will wear, what we will eat–yet so often these are exactly the things that create worry and anxiety in our lives. *'God knows you need these things before you ask'* (Matt 6:8).

Since we have died and risen in Christ, God wants us to share in his approach and live in his rest. Thus we become an insouciant believer, able to live in the freedom from concern that he promised us. Insouciant: relaxed and happy, with no feelings of worry and guilt. When Jesus spoke in the synagogue at Nazareth he was not just helping out the attendant when he read the passage from Isaiah (Luke 4:17-19); he was announcing that his very incarnation was declaring a new era of favour, an application of Jubilee to all! The news of God's goodness was now broadcast, and the 'poor' would immediately see the relevance. Those trapped in addiction, or bound by laws of religious performance, weighed down by perfectionism–imprisoned by the D.I.Y. approach to life–would taste freedom for the first time. Blindness, both physical and psychological, would meet the Healer. He declared 'the time of the Lord's favour has come'... and sitting down–which was an indication of authority–he boldly announced, *'The scripture you've just heard has been fulfilled this very day!'* We have a choice: will we live in this?

Apparently English speakers learned the word 'insouciance' from the French in the 1700s. It referred to a relaxed and calm state: a feeling of not worrying about anything. This may seem idealistic but there is good biblical precedent for such an approach. Maybe this is what Paul was envisioning in Philippians 4:6-7. In contemporary speech, we could say, 'Talk through everything at the beginning of the day or before things happen. And (if you cannot understand it all) be thankful for what you can see God is doing. God's peace becomes the hallmark of the day.'

Life is not always easy, however, and relationships can become complicated. All of us, from time to time, can feel overwhelmed by circumstances. How do we approach life in such a way as to retain a healthy insouciance, when surrounded by challenges? So much depends on our mindset, hence the call for *metanoia*, thinking differently. I once heard how a family who had lost a child would approach the anniversary positively, saying, 'It is best to attack the day rather than be overwhelmed by it.' It can be helpful to develop a strategy to deal with recurring issues of the mind. These suggestions may help:

Reset at the beginning of each day. We can forget who we are now in Christ when we feel we're 'swimming against the tide.' Yet to remind ourselves of the Gospel each day is essential. *'My old self has been crucified with Christ. It is no longer I who live, but Christ lives in me. So I live in this earthly body by trusting in the Son of God, who loved me and gave himself for me'* (Gal 2:20). Many modern translations render this as 'faith in Christ' but most scholars are agreed that that the Greek is much better stated as the 'faith of Christ'. The small change in preposition gives a huge change in meaning. The use of 'in' puts us back onto ourselves to drum up enough faith–when would we ever know what would be enough?– while the 'faith of Christ' acknowledges that it was only ever by his faithfulness that we were saved. His faith was perfect in every way! C.S. Lewis said that we have not so much need to be taught as to be reminded ... we definitely need to be reminded of our new state in union with Christ, because of his finished work. It may help to have to hand a number of key verses about who we are now in Christ: remember to view all scripture though the lens of Christ.

Interrupt negative patterns. We are all different, but are we prone to dwell on negative thoughts: what someone said, should we have done something differently, are we achieving anything? If so, it can be helpful to engage our bodies in some activity, distract ourselves, help someone (thus taking the focus off ourselves). I once heard how an experienced teacher used much in healing would sometimes feel overloaded, so would take himself off into the garden and do some mundane weeding or pruning for a day or two. We have for too long elevated the mind over a holistic understanding of our being; often it is very therapeutic to work with our hands, or with animals and the natural world. We read we are to *'take every thought captive to Christ'* (2 Cor 10:5). If we struggle with the thoughts that sometimes arrive, we can just acknowledge, 'Oh, there's that thought again,' and let it go, without dwelling on it. It is not part of our True Self.

Live in the present. As has already been mentioned, we tend to live in the past or the future. That is not to say that those things are irrelevant, but if we can reset our focus to enjoy the moment we will find each day much more pleasurable. Jesus acknowledged that we will have trouble in this world, but also said *'So don't worry about tomorrow, for tomorrow will bring its own worries. Today's trouble is enough for today'* (Matt 6:34). Even though the washing machine may have broken down and the car may need an expensive repair, these things are like the undulating surface on a varied landscape; underneath there is the rich strata with enduring seams of God's love and provision. We 'sink back into Jesus' and live in trust that the Father, Son and Holy Spirit will never abandon us.

Live thankfully. It is amazing how consideration of all the things we have to be thankful for can change our outlook–if we're having a bad day, start with the smallest thing, like the shoes we have to wear. Many around the world go barefoot. Whatever is going on, we can even decide to smile! In fact, thankfulness is a recurring theme in the scriptures, *'So thank God for his marvellous love, for his miracle mercy to the children he loves'* (Psalm 107:21 MSG). The Lord loves a grateful heart, and we see Jesus giving thanks for food and for the way the Father has revealed himself. *'Giving thanks is a sacrifice that truly honours Me'* (Psalm 50:23 NLT).

Live in community. Living in Christ was never intended to be an individualistic experience, just 'me and Jesus'. We were born from above into a body, a household, a new form of 'temple' that God indwells. We can avoid becoming inward-looking, developing warped notions about ourselves and others or taking rigid positions on issues that ignore our basic humanity. When Jesus spoke of building his church in Matthew 16, he was not referring to an organisation. He was rather seeing a living organism that carried his life throughout its veins, built on the revelation of who he is and existing through the covenant love of God. We need others to remind us of who we really are in Christ! And they need us too–people sometimes say, 'I stopped going to church because I wasn't getting anything out of it.' Well, firstly we cannot really go to church, as we **are** the *ecclesia*, and secondly, if we approach this with a consumer mindset, we have misunderstood completely. Our contribution is a vital aspect of the life of the body, and as we participate, we find we too are encouraged. It is also intended to be fun! The early church called their communion times 'love feasts'. The benefits of belonging to this kind of loving family are amazing. However if the local expression of church you have been used to does not convey the basic truths that we have been sharing regarding the finished work of the cross and the rest that God wishes us to dwell in, and instead has a religious culture of 'try harder' or performance, it may be healthier to seek out some other people to gather with who can share with you in this Trinitarian life.

None of these suggestions should be seen as 'something you have to do' to be loved and known by God. You are starting from the finished line in Christ: the life you live is one of exploration, understanding and unveiling. It is not one of progressive acceptance. 'We were saved not for probation, but for education' teaches Baxter Kruger, i.e. not to find out whether we are good enough, but rather to understand the depth of what Christ has accomplished on our behalf. Luther said that the Gospel is not about how we can become justified or righteous, it is rather a declaration of how Christ made us justified and righteous.

It can take time to detox from a religious mindset! It is like a pernicious weed that spreads ... we think we have pulled it up, only to find it popping up again. Give yourself time, immerse yourself in the finished work of the Lover of your Soul, the Saviour of the World. His intention all along is that you dwell in his ultimate rest.

ELEVEN | Conclusion: The Beautiful Gospel

There is a simplicity about the Gospel that even a child can understand! Jesus emphasised this in Matthew 18 to his muddled disciples, who had been concerned about status and prestige. Yet though simple, the Gospel is also many layered and incredibly woven in a depth of revelation reaching back through the scriptures to the Genesis account in the garden. It is both simple and yet so profound that the wisest Christian mystics could devote their whole lives to contemplating the wonder of God.

> From all eternity, long before you were born and became a part of history, you existed in God's heart. Long before your parents admired you or your friends acknowledged your gifts or your teachers, colleagues and employers encouraged you, you were already 'chosen'. The eyes of love had seen you as precious, as of infinite beauty, as of eternal value. When love chooses, it chooses with a perfect sensitivity for the unique beauty of the chosen one, and it chooses without making anyone else feel excluded.[56] (Henri Nouwen)

Unfortunately, the Gospel has often been presented as a proposition, when in fact it is an announcement! It is not a set of conditions that need to be fulfilled before we can meet God. Rather it is the wonder of light breaking into our darkness, announcing that God himself has provided the answer (even before we've thought of the question). Zechariah spoke over the infant John the Baptist, *'Because of God's tender mercy, the morning light from heaven is about to break upon*

---

[56] Henri Nouwen, *Life of the Beloved* (Crossroad Publishing, 2002), 45.

us, to give light to those who sit in darkness and in the shadow of death, and to guide us into the path of peace' (Luke 1:78-79). The Passion Translation renders this as *'the splendour-light of heaven's glorious sunrise.'* We were in a desperate place, 'running *around in circles' ... 'But then, oh happy day. It was the generosity of God and his fondness for mankind that dawned on us like a shaft of light. Our days of darkness were over. Light shone everywhere and we became aware: God rescued the human race'* (Titus 3:4 MIR).

Therefore, at the birth of Jesus the angel announced to the astonished shepherds, *'Don't be afraid! ... I bring you good news that will bring great joy to all people. The Saviour–yes, the Messiah–has been born today ....'* (From Luke 2:10-11). As the Mirror says it, *'Listen! I have the most wonderful announcement to make – this will lead to the great encounter of the most joyful bliss for every single person on the planet!'* No wonder the skies then erupted with angel choirs in a blaze of glorious light! If the version of the Gospel you have heard doesn't sound like good news, then you've not heard the Gospel.

Karl Barth famously taught that God is so great, so 'other', that he cannot be 'discovered' by our efforts – he can only choose to reveal himself. And the Godhead has chosen to do this through the man, Jesus Christ, the Son of God. The Word of God, Jesus, born as one of us, as a human being entering into all we experience in this darkened world, would reveal to us the Light, the true nature of a God who is a perfect Father and has always loved us. *'The Word gave life to everything that was created, and his life brought light to everyone. The light shines in the darkness, and the darkness can never extinguish it [or has not understood it]'* (John 1:4-5). The Message says, *'the darkness couldn't put it out.'* The darkness represents mankind's ignorance of our redeemed identity and our futile attempts to justify ourselves by our own efforts. Jesus cut through that with his message of humble, self-giving, cruciform love. In so doing he wasn't saying, 'Do these ten things and you'll be acceptable for heaven.' Rather, Jesus, the one true human, represented us, as John Crowder explains:

> Most have never taken the leap of realizing our spirituality is based not upon what we *do*, but upon what Jesus *did*. Even fewer can comprehend that it is based upon Who Jesus *is*. In the incarnation, God has folded our humanity into His very identity as God. His incarnate Person *is* the unity of God with His creation. His personal incarnation is also cosmic, and though united to all it is personalized to us. This solid fact remains: Jesus *is* your relationship with God.[57]

It is clear that if Jesus should go through this life and then yield it up to death, everything and everyone would be affected. T. F. Torrance wrote, 'Since he is the eternal Word of God by whom and through whom all things that are made are made, and in whom the whole universe of visible and invisible realities coheres and hangs together, and since in him divine and human natures are inseparably united, then the secret of every man, whether he believes it or not, is bound up with Jesus for it is in him that human contingent existence has been grounded and secured.'[58] The implications of this God-with-us man dying for us and then being raised to life sends light waves through the universe!

Jesus Christ healed us of the 'disease' of sin, a mindset of separation from God that had been spawned through distrust and the doubt that

---

[57] John Crowder: *Advent Day 4 Meditation* (online, 2023).
[58] T. F. Torrance, Trinitarian Faith: The Evangelical Theology of the Ancient Catholic Faith (Continuum International Publishing, 2003), 182-183.

he was truly good (resulting in bad fruit that harmed what God had originally intended). We were in a state of slavery, but he freed us once and for all. He 'laid the axe to the root', ensuring that we were not longer bound by Adam's choice. All the guilt and shame of our condition was borne by him on the cross, so that in exchange we might enjoy the innocence, the 'right-with-God-ness' of the Last Adam.

In addition, in rising from the dead, he broke the power and fear of death from our lives! Jesus became the example of us, the new man that God had restored–this was in fact God's plan from the beginning:

God knew what he was doing from the very beginning. He decided from the outset to shape the lives of those who love him along the same lines as the life of his Son. The Son stands first in the line of humanity he restored. We see the original and intended shape of our lives there in him (Romans 8:29 Message).

What the Trinity of Love brought about was our union with Christ, that we might now live *in* and *through* him for eternity. Aware of our oneness with him, we can participate with him by sharing the message of reconciliation and demonstrating it through *agape* love.[59] We find ourselves partaking in the works the Father has prepared beforehand, that carry all the qualities of the Kingdom of God. These are woven together like an incredible cosmic tapestry in which we see

---

[59] Original Greek: ἀγάπη (agápē) Agape is often defined as unconditional, sacrificial love. Agape is the kind of love that is felt by a person willing to do anything for another, including sacrificing themselves, without expecting anything in return (Dictionary.com).

what Wm. Paul Young refers to as 'God's redeeming genius' at work, with 'God-instances' revealing his purpose and glory.[60]

The Christian life is not one of striving for performance or perfection. Rather it is an overflow of Jesus' life–a life sourced in him–that expresses itself through 'good fruit'. As those abiding in the vine, we are created to carry his life ... and large juicy grapes are the natural result. As those immersed in the Spirit, listening to the Spirit, we find ourselves displaying the glory of the Kingdom in a myriad of ways that only God could orchestrate.

My eldest brother is a farmer who 20 years ago gave up dairying and transferred part of his land over to growing cider apples. He planted 15,000 trees on 50 acres, and each year they produce over 1200 tons of apples, enough amazingly for 45 full articulated lorry-loads (or semis to our American friends). Although he tends the orchards, the fruit just comes as a natural result of the budding branches connected to the trees.

As we rest in Christ, we too shall produce abundant fruit! Rest is not inaction, but action flowing from rest. Jesus says in John 15:2 that the Father prunes ('lifts up and dresses') every branch that is not producing, so that it may keep on bearing more fruit ('more and more')–Francois du Toit points out in reference to this passage that the Word is God's pruning tool, incarnated in sonship. In our seamless union with Christ, the sap of life flows up through us and we participate actively in his wonderful work of reconciliation, healing

---

[60] Wm. Paul Young is the author of the bestselling novels *The Shack, Cross Roads* and *Eve* plus an exploration of the wrong-headed ideas we sometimes have in *Lies we Believe About God*. He used this phrase, 'God's redeeming genius' in one of his many interviews.

and love. And with typical use of hyperbole, Jesus says that anything else would just be firewood–and that is *not* what we are!

'Grace infuses you. Grace is a Person who possesses and fuels you.'[61] True rest comes from knowing and flowing from a heart united with His. This is the rest we all need!

Here's a great quote by Matt Spinks: 'One of the most challenging things for us to understand as humans is true rest .... It's a divine grace proceeding from the intimate knowledge of Jesus and what He has accomplished. I get to be myself, not competing or comparing, but just being, flowing and participating in the joy of living ... loving what He's called me to, so never really working a day in my life, even as I work. Living absolutely secure that there's nothing I need to force, no one I need to save, nothing to truly fear, no love I need to earn. He is giving each of us that gift of His rest today. And it's more than we can comprehend. It's more than we know how to receive. Thank you, Holy Spirit, for waking us up to Jesus' deep and wide REST!'[62]

Holy Spirit testifies in our hearts of the peace of God, not in future worries, but in the present moment.
'Then Jesus said, "Come to me, all of you who are weary and carry heavy burdens, and I will give you rest"' (Matthew 11:28).

'I am leaving you with a gift—peace of mind and heart. And the peace I give is a gift the world cannot give. So don't be troubled or afraid' (John 14:27).

---

[61] John Crowder, at the *Telos* week, Cornwall 2022.
[62] Matt Spinks 'Rest - Part Three' teaching at the Jubilee Online Church 2024.

For He is the Very Rest.
God wishes to be known,
And it pleases Him that
We rest in Him;
For all that is beneath Him
Will never satisfy us.
Therefore no soul is rested
Til it is emptied of all things
That are made.
When for love of Him,
It is empty,
The soul can
Receive His deep rest.

Julian of Norwich[63]

---

[63] Quoted by Roger Housden, *For Lovers of God Everywhere* (Hay House, Inc. 2009), 188.

APPENDIX ONE | Wild Wellness!

Wellness and rest

By Rachel Hewitt

"Working, running, spinning, busy, busy, busy ... He makes me lie down and rest." John Mark Pantana 'Rest'.

In society today it is very true that people are searching for rest, wellness, peace, a sense of balance and of well-being. In fact, there is a multi-dollar industry to help fill the place of longing, desiring, searching and restlessness in the human soul. We do live in one of the busiest times in history. There is so much vying for our attention, with many situations causing both stress and cortisol to rise in our body. However, within the wellness industry there are many components that can help, and it is most beneficial to entwine these together with God's intention that we be at peace in him.

Ultimately, our wellness comes from drawing from and living in that wellspring of life which gives us rest. As Matt Spinks put it in a meditation, we are 'resting in the wine vine', the source and root of our lives.[64] Our bodies have been designed for rest, perfect peace, shalom. We were never created for a constant cortisol fight/flight life of survival. We were created and placed in a garden for balance, life

---

[64] Matt & Katie Spinks podcast: The Firehouse Chronicles *Mystic Meditations– abiding in the Wine Vine*, March 2020 (www.thefirehouseprojects.com).

and to move and do things from a place of peace. *'For in him we live and move and have our being'* (Acts 17 v 28 NIV).
Philippians 4 v 7 in the Mirror version says:

> *And in this place of worship and gratitude you will witness how the peace of God within you echoes the awareness of your oneness in Christ Jesus beyond the reach of any thought that could possibly unsettle you. Just like the sentry guard secures a city, watching out in advance for the first signs of any possible threat, your deepest feelings and the tranquillity of your thoughts are fully guarded there.* (The word *uperecho* translates, echoes ... beyond the reach of. And φρουρέω *phroureō*, guarding the gates of the city. This peace is not measured by external circumstances, it is residing deeply in the innermost parts of your being. We are not talking about a fragile sense of peace that can easily be disturbed; one that we have to fabricate ourselves; this is God's peace; the peace that God himself enjoys. This peace surpasses all the confines of our own reasonings, and floods our hearts and minds with a tranquillity that takes charge of our emotions and wellbeing in fragile times.)

There is a deep well of steadfast, secure peace that we can connect to, and that we dwell in. The peace, as Francois du Toit says, that 'God himself enjoys'. This is found in the resonance of our oneness in Christ, more secure than anything that could disturb our rest. Here is a pool of peace that never ends and that saturates us to the core. Life's traumas or pains can sometimes cause us to see this through a warped lens, but as we allow those to 'be' and embrace them into Jesus' wholeness, seeing that those places are whole in our oneness in him, light will start to reflect again bringing hope and balance back to hurt places. Security, peace and safety etc are part of the beautiful core of who God is, and he can't be anything other than who he is. He never changes, he is steadfast and true. Totally trustworthy. Hebrews 6 v 15-19 speaks about God's secure character as 'an unshakable hope'!

It is so precious, the way God loves our humanity. As we find our ultimate security in his steadfast peace, I think there is a beautiful place where these entwine: resting in God, being in his peace, his source and his balance, and then incorporating rhythms and practises into our lives as tools which help ground our being and our body.

I am a dancer and graduated in studying Wellness Therapies with Lifestyle Advice. In this I have seen that there is a space to draw all these things together: the supernatural and the natural.

In the holistic wellness industry this ability to restore to a place of balance and peace is called *homeostasis*. The dictionary definition of this is:

> *Homeostasis n. the physiological process by which the internal systems of the body (e.g. blood pressure, body temperature, acid-base balance) are maintained at equilibrium, despite variations in the external conditions. —* ***homeostatic*** *adj.*

Homeostasis is a place where the body is completely balanced despite what is happening around it and has the ability to maintain/come back to balance when stress comes its way. This is the place the body heals and restores itself from stress, where it has resilience.

Dr Pete Sulack[65] states that 'a body at rest wins every single time'.[66] He is a Christian chiropractor in the United States who has been advocating the need to restore homeostasis to the body, so that when stress happens our bodies have the tools to come back into balance. This then helps the body remain in wellness and health.

Stress is a natural occurrence in the body; not only big stresses in life like trauma or serious situations, even a busy day or a virus can cause stress on the body. However, our bodies have been so amazingly, intricately created by God that they are designed to cope with stress; then they want to re balance and to be well – we are created for wild wellness! (Some practical ways to help our natural body come into balance and peace will follow.)

Beauty

I also believe interwoven into this is the fact we are made for beauty. To gaze upon God's absorbing beauty, to reflect it and immerse within it. The world craves beauty, doing everything it can to buy it, create it and to be surrounded by it. Beauty is reflected in many things. One of these is in Creation. When in Genesis the Bible records, 'God said it was good', this could also be translated as 'God said it was beautiful'. Gen 1:27 also states that we are created in the image of God, in his image and likeness.

---

[65] Dr Pete Sulack's studies on the effects of stress, coupled with testimonials from patients and attention in medical communities have garnered him the title of 'America's Leading Stress Expert'.

[66] Stated in a Liz Wright podcast *Live Your Best Life*, Episode 148, *Living from a place of Rest* with Dr Pete Sulack.

Scientists have discovered that when we spend time in nature and beauty our bodies relax, cortisol levels drop, and we balance. In fact, we are really made for beauty, which is why walking in a forest listening to bird song or picking flowers causes our body to flourish in wellness! Why not try it right now, step outside your door to the garden or a local park, pause and breathe. Take in bird songs, the sound of the wind, the glittering of sunlight and become aware of your body relaxing and your breathing steadying.

In her book 'Spa Living'[67], Sunamita Lim describes the experience of connecting with spa treatments, their ambiance and holistic wellbeing focus as 'regain(ing) *hozho*, or 'walking in beauty ' as the Navajos call it.' Lim describes how spa living has helped her reconnect with herself and ground her in love and faith like a child, giving her overall a wonderful sense of well-being. I believe spas, wellness places and routines like meditating help us connect to beauty. Beauty is often seen to symbolise truth, yet unfortunately in society so often what is shown as beauty isn't truth, it is twisted by fake news, filters and airbrushing.

There is a captivating beauty in God which is reflected both in his creation and within us.

> For just as God is infinitely the greatest Being, so also we agree that he is infinitely the most beautiful and excellent: all the beauty anywhere in the whole creation is only a reflection of the beams radiating from that infinitely bright and glorious Being. God's beauty is infinitely more valuable than that of all

[67] Sunamita Lim, Spa Living: Ideas, Tips & Recipes for Revitalizing Body-Mind-Spirit (Gibbs M. Smith Inc, 2007), 14.

> other beings, because of how virtuous he is and of how great he is. (Jonathan Edwards)[68]

I do not agree with all of Edward's theology, however I do love this quote focusing on God's infinite beauty, radiating from his very Being!

That WOW in the wonder of nature, the skill in the colour or line of a painting, or a song that touches the resonance in our heart ... the reflection looking back at you in the mirror. Yes, maybe the hardest place to 'see' that wow clearly is through your natural eyes ... but you are created in his image, you incarnate his wow, his beauty, his delight – and you shine with it. You are no less of a wow than that sunset that took your breath away. God himself leaps and dances, singing over you, you are His poem[69]. WOW, WOW, WOW!! Don't allow the 'world' to bargain with your wow reflection. Those harsh words and feelings come from pain. The thorns which try to protect are counterfeits of reflections, hiding the truth. I have experienced that too, the words or actions that cut to our core causing us to cover ourselves with a shell, as the rejection-wound says 'hide' and accept the fact that you are dull and unpleasant.

However, this is *not* truth. Take a deep breath and hold his hand to lead you into the reality of your reflection. As we wow in his wonder, we are filled with his beauty which fills deep rivers inside of us.
"I am a reflection of His beauty; I am beautiful outside and in".

Melissa Johnson says, 'So often societal beauty has us running after that which doesn't bring us life. It promises what it can't deliver.'

---

[68] Jonathan Edwards A Dissertation Concerning the Nature of True Virtue, 1765.
[69] From the Greek word *poema*: God's workmanship.

Take time to immerse yourself in magnificence, walk by the sea, watch a sunset, listed to your favourite song and as you connect to that beauty remember you also reflect that beauty too and allow that to settle in your heart; and grow, so that it becomes a new thought... a moulding of *metanoia* in your mind. So that you will look in the mirror and see it reflecting back too: 'I am a reflection of His beauty; I am beautiful outside and in.'

In the words of Godfrey Birtill's song:

> Do you believe what I believe about you? Do you know what I know to be true? ... You are beautiful, so precious too, you're irreplaceable and unique, created for this intimacy, and forever we belong together.[70]

Pop this song on loud and on repeat and let those words sink in deep!!

We are all unique

We all have the unique thumbprint of God: created to mirror and reflect a facet of who he is, and have an inimitable, beautiful relationship which no one else will ever experience. My body will never respond to life or situations in the way yours will. I don't believe there is a cookie-cutter, one size fits all approach to wellness, which is why holistic wellbeing is so powerful; it is person centred and finds ways that will support the body in its uniqueness. Nevertheless, there are some things which help all of us, as they are good for our bodies.

---

[70] Godfrey Birtill (Thankyou Music, UK) © available on the album *Two Thousand Years Ago We Bled Into One,* 2012.

Here are a few examples of things that can be easily included into our routine, which help to naturally lower stress within the body:

Walking or being in nature – as mentioned before, our bodies are created to respond positively to nature, reducing cortisol and bringing our being into rest.

Generosity and kindness – did you know that they have a massive impact on our health? Dr David Hamilton[71] has studied the way kindness affects people. He says that kindness actually has a physical effect on our heart, the immune system and throughout the body[72] reducing stress. Kindness can be as simple as sending someone a message saying how much you appreciate their friendship or giving the next person in the queue at a coffee shop your full stamp card for a free coffee.

Contentment and positive meditation – meditating on truth and having a thankful heart actually assist us in maintaining a sense of rest. There are always things we would like, or things to pray for. However, when we can take a breath and balance this with being content in our heart, stress decreases. Finding contentment in God, knowing he has everything in hand, he is faithful and loves us completely, is a way to find this contentment in life.

---

[71] Dr David Hamilton left a career in industry to write books and educate people in how they can harness their mind and emotions to improve their mental and physical health. He is the author of 11 books, including the bestseller, *The Five Side Effects of Kindness* (Hay House, 2017).

[72] Dr David Hamilton, The Little Book of Kindness: Connect with others, be happier, transform your life (Octopus publishing group, 2019).

If you find this hard to start, just begin by writing one thing you are thankful for every morning and evening. It doesn't need to be profound, just 'I am thankful for my morning coffee' is perfect. Let that new seed of thankfulness grow within you and it will flourish, then soon you will be writing out more.

Moving, stretching, Pilates etc – it is important to move our body as it helps activate our lymphatic system, enabling it to wash out toxins from the body. It also supports the body in getting rid of tension, built up emotion and trauma. If you're not a massive fan of exercise, just find a five-minute beginner 'stretching or relaxing movement' video on YouTube. It is amazing how much better it can make us feel afterwards.

Drink plenty of water! – Water also helps to wash out toxins from the body helping our bodies stay healthy. This in turn also supports *homeostasis* in the body as hydration keeps all our body systems running at their optimum level.

Self-love – Be kind to yourself! Do things that give you life. Find a new hobby, set aside time for a present one, and enjoy it to the max. Take a bath, light a candle, cook a new recipe, garden, write a journal ... the list is endless! As we give ourselves time to do things we love, our body relaxes and dopamine increases, making us feel happier and also more content. If we are continually running on empty, our bodies produce more cortisol, and we constantly live life out of 'fight or flight' mode (or our sympathetic nervous system). When we practise doing things that give us life and being kind to ourselves, stopping for a moment to focus on God and His goodness, it helps us to connect to our parasympathetic nervous system (rest and digest mode). This system brings us back into balance.

Speak kindly over yourself! – Did you know that as we speak out, we create? Just like our Father God when he spoke and it happened, he has given us the same ability to speak things into existence. Listen to your inward or outward conversation with yourself. You are beautifully created, not stupid, crazy, unlovable, a disaster, ugly or clumsy etc. Ask God what he thinks of you – What words would he use to describe you? I know 100% that it won't be any words in the list above! Do you need to forgive yourself or someone else connected to the words you speak over yourself? Start speaking the opposite and see what happens!

Conclusion

When weaving these together–resting in God's unshakable, continuous peace and practising everyday methods of reducing stress–we find a balanced place of flourishing in harmony, wholeness and relaxation. I love Psalm 23, especially the way David writes about God being a trustworthy and safe place where we can rest, relax and know no lack. Pastures green and luscious, waters still and refreshing, surrounded by his protection and safety!

Close your eyes. Take three deep, slow breaths, in and out. Scan your body internally and see how you are doing. Invite Jesus to say anything and give any place of discomfort or anxiety to him. Ask him to envelope those places. Hold his hand and let him guide you into new ways of seeing yourself, with wellness and beauty. He is faithful. Let his love warm your heart and surround you now. Open your eyes. All is good. He has got you.

APPENDIX TWO | Meditations on Rest

A meditation for healing and wholeness

By Marjory Morrow

Get into a comfortable position. Take a few deep breaths, inhaling to the count of four, holding and exhaling to the count of five. Begin to do this a few times: inhaling to the count of four, exhaling to the count of five, and as you are breathing, allow your body to relax.

Feel all tension easing away from your head, and relax your jaw, the tension leaving your neck and shoulders, allow your shoulders to drop, your arms and your hands to relax and your fingers to just gently curl upwards as you lay them on your lap. Allow all tension from across your back, and across your stomach, and your hips, to leave, and allow all tension from your hips, knees and calves and ankles to go. And finally feel your feet and feel every last ounce of tension leave through your feet, till your body feels completely relaxed.

Now bring you attention to your breath and allow your breath to come back into a natural and relaxed rhythm. Focus your attention on the inhale–goes in through your nose, and the exhale–goes out through your mouth. Don't worry about thoughts, just allow them to come, and as they come allow them then to go, and continue to bring your attention back to your breath.

Remind yourself that you are one with God, that you are one with Abba, one with Jesus, one with the Holy Spirit; in him you move, and you live, and you have your being.

Feel the complete union that you have with Christ, in God, surrounded and held by Holy Spirit. Right now, see the *shalom* peace of God as a great big vat of oil above your head, and see that oil slowly being released:

> down upon your head,
> gently covering your face and your neck,
> feeling it moving across your shoulders,
> down your arms and chest,
> down your back and around your stomach.
> Feel that warm, fragrant, healing oil moving down,
> across your hips,
> down your legs,
> around your knees,
> down your calves,
> around your feet.

Feel yourself completely surrounded, completely covered in this beautiful, fragrant, healing oil...

Say into yourself:

> Every cell in my body is completely swimming in love, surrounded by love. Kept and made new in love. Every last

atom within me, every last part of me, down to the smallest particle, completely surrounded in love–vibrating with the energy and frequency of love.

All dis-ease and dis-function is completely dissolved, destroyed and obliterated in this love! I see every part of my body restored and renewed in complete perfection. When Christ died, I died, when he arose, I arose, complete fulness of life is mine.

I am the image of Christ. When Papa looks at me, he only sees Jesus. My mind and my thoughts are completely renewed in Christ. I have the mind of Christ. All my old habits, toxic thought patterns, traumas, bad experiences in life that are stored in my brain or my body–right now those thoughts, those places in my body are being completely purged, completely cleansed. Every trace of them is being destroyed and removed for ever. There is no landing strip any longer for any disease, disfunction, any self-loathing or self-hatred.

I am adored. I am valuable, precious, completely loved, completely wanted, absolutely desired. The reality is that right now I am complete and whole, lacking nothing–and I am free from all condemnation. The slate is wiped completely clean and I am pure and holy and blameless. I have access to the Divine Nature. I have been given every spiritual blessing in heavenly places in Christ Jesus. I am a co-heir with Christ. All things are mine.

There is no apparent difficult circumstance, disease or dysfunction in my body, no apparent lack … that is really just that, an apparition, something appearing as real that really is false.

Cos the truth is I lack nothing, no good thing is withheld form me, whether that be healing, whether that be good relationships, whether that be dreams fulfilled. No good thing is withheld from me! And the greater truth and the greater reality is that which I declare to be in the I AM.

I am a precious daughter, I am a precious son, I am abundant in every way. Fruit of the Spirit shows up in my life; I have love, I have joy, I have peace, I have patience, I have goodness, I have gentleness, I have self-control … and against such things there is no law.

I bring up into my thinking anything that is causing a lack of peace in my life right now and I just allow myself to look at it without judging it, and now I choose within my mind to see it as completely resolved, I choose to see what the outcome is, in Christ. I choose to see Jesus looking at it, smiling, saying, 'I can fix that, I've totally got this, *you've* totally got this, just see it as I see it.'

And allow yourself, in your thinking to see the outcome in a new way, see your body completely restored, see yourself doing things that you perhaps couldn't do before. See yourself ten years down the line, healthy, well, abundant, living a full and rich life. Allow God to take every place of fear–completely destroy it in his peace. See it all burned up in the white-hot heat of his love and of his peace.

Now allow yourself to be taken by the hand and led, led down a pathway that leads to the River of Life, pastures where your soul is renewed, restored. See yourself walking with God in the cool of the day. Allow him now to talk with you, to even just sit and be with him wordlessly in contemplation.

Allow Holy Spirit just to move, to speak, whatever comes naturally to you, feel it now, hear it now, see it now... And when you're ready, begin to bring yourself to a place where you just gently open your eyes. You are still feeling that hope and that joy and that love and that peace that has been imparted to you, and as you rise and get on with the rest of you day–or even as you perhaps now go to bed–take with you that sense of love, peace, assurance, joy.

There is absolutely no separation between you and God. You are perfectly entangled into one. Amen. Amen.

A recording of Marjory reading this over music is available on the website www.wellsprings.uk.net

A short meditation on rest

By David Hewitt

So, I see you are feeling stressed! A flurry of insidious lies and half-truths have besieged your mind. Stop ... listen ... come aside, take a deep breath and 'reset.'

You are, right now, this very moment, the delight of my eyes! Everything necessary for your complete acceptance and rest in me has already been accomplished. When I died, you were co-crucified with me, and when I rose, you were co-raised too: today you live in me through my faithfulness and love. In fact, I dealt with this even before the earth came into being. I am fully satisfied that your redemption was complete, without your assistance!

Your 'need to perform' died with me. I deal in reality, what is authentic and true. I am not dismayed by all the loose ends and unresolved issues that concern you. Lay aside any thought of comparison with others–you are uniquely fashioned–in fact I have made you free to be fully who you are. And stop replaying those conversations in your mind and second-guessing what others were thinking about you. It really doesn't matter! Let it go.

Consider where I have now placed you, in union with me. I am now the environment you dwell in, the land you are able to flourish in. Explore with me the extent of this place; there are exciting new areas to discover, open vistas, fresh perspectives. Unparalleled beauty exists for us to enjoy together, new textures, patterns and shapes as well as the most pleasing scents and sounds. You can stretch out wide in me, exploring the infinite dimensions of my love. You are safe here, I am your life now, your new existence.

You were not made to carry the woes of the world on your shoulders. Allow me to carry that. Instead, just delight in following my prompts, my leading; learn the things that are important to me. Remember, there's no condemnation in this new life we share–I took that all on myself. And the ruler of this world was condemned in me. He has no hold over you any longer; only lies and half-truths to try and steal your peace.

However, I told you, 'My peace I give to you'–and I will not take it away. I have also given you my authority– you are seated with me in heavenly places, even as I am seated at the right hand of the Father. So, fear not, you are forever included in me, surrounded with my love.

I have given you my ultimate rest.

APPENDIX THREE | Some prayers

A prayer to live in Ultimate Rest

Thank you, Father, Son and Holy Spirit, that your intention for me was to dwell within you in a place of ultimate rest, the environment of life and joy that you created for us when you rested from your work.

Jesus, you are my Eternal Sabbath–by living my life and dying my death, you finished the work of healing and redemption–so I can 'sink back' into you.

Thank you that I am declared innocent, a new creation formed in love.

You took on the very dust of the universe you created, and with utmost humility and love-beyond-measure, gave me your very Self–that as I feed on you through the covenanted meal and a life that becomes prayer, you sustain me!

I drink, as it were, from the Divine breast, fed and nurtured to maturity by the Life of the Ages.

Thank you for making provision for all I need in advance and yet involving me in the creative process–a life of partnership in pleasure as you designed from the beginning. This is the work of rest.

Thank you that you remind me moment by moment who I am. Help me to take those micro-moments today, to pause and reflect on who I am now in you and see 'the way of my being aligned with the truth of my being,' the Last Adam, Jesus Christ.

In the name of the Father, Son and Holy Spirit!

A prayer when everything seems to be going wrong

Father, Son and Holy Spirit, I am in a really difficult place and cannot understand why it seems that 'the wheels are coming off' at the moment. Nothing seems to be going right.

I thank you that you know me better than I know myself, Lord, and have always known me since the beginning of time.

I remember that you formed me in my mother's womb and created me as a free, wonderful person, bearing your image only 'a little lower than the gods'–free to love and choose and displaying your glory–and that you do not control me or the world I live in like a director of a theatrical production or a mechanic with a machine.

Yet I know too, Lord, that you are sovereign and sustain the universe by your all-powerful word, and that though the present order was damaged by mankind seeking darkness rather than light, yet everything necessary for our wholeness and healing was satisfied and finished through your work.

You live as the One New Man and I live in you, united and made whole. You are patient and compassionate. You are my Best Friend and my Good Shepherd–a redeeming genius–and the kindest I will ever know.

Thank you that you are not shocked by what I say by my strength of feeling, but you love me completely!

Thank you that you do not ask me to 'tick some more boxes' or perform better; in your abiding, covenanted love you settled forever the issue of my worthiness and acceptance before the Godhead.

You are my righteousness and my salvation. By your faithfulness I am now included in Christ, one with you, held forever in love.

I understand that the present situation is not a punishment, and you are not viewing me from afar with an angry frown. Rather you are within me in all I go through, and I am hidden in you.

I pray for this situation to change, and I see myself flourishing with new energy and clarity, and I receive your wisdom. You have given me your authority and your peace.

Above all Lord I rest in your abiding, covenant love, and choose to trust you now for this moment, as I live present in you.

In the name of the Father, Son and Holy Spirit!

A prayer when in confusion or mental stress

Lord, I feel the things I'm going through are like waves threatening to engulf me. I can't seem to hear you or understand what is happening.

You remind me that you call to yourself all who are weighed down with burdens, and offer in exchange your gift of rest.

Being 'yoked to you' reminds me that I am not living this life on my own, but have been brought into union with you, sharing your life of complete faithfulness. I don't have to drum up enough faith to succeed–instead I participate with you in your absolute sufficiency!

And as I am united with you, I realise I'm united with all in Christ–a living functioning part of the body. You are my pace setter as we make this journey together–help me to keep in step with you, living one day at a time and not trying to rush ahead.

'A bruised reed you will not break and a smouldering wick you will not snuff out.' You are always patient with me, never disillusioned or disappointed, as you know me completely, dying for me before I'd ever thought of you.

I remember that through the Son of God you have made full provision for me, so that I may 'sink' into him, his love, his kindness and long-suffering, without any sense of guilt, regret or shame–you took all that on yourself and buried it in the tomb, giving me instead your life and wholeness.

Help me participate in your sustaining mercy and grace, 'feeding' on you even when I can't understand or feel it. I remind myself that I am not designed to carry the weight of the world on my shoulders, nor even the decisions or thoughts of other people, but instead feed daily from you, the Tree of Life.

I let go now the demands and pressures I've taken on, the comparisons with others, the judgements I've made, and remember that I died with you, co-crucified and then co-raised, and this new life you have for me is one of full acceptance and perfect love.

I hear the Father saying over me, 'You are my son/daughter in whom I'm well pleased.'

I remind myself that your approval is all I need, and that you made up your mind about me before the world even began and intended from the start to make me whole in the Son of God.

Thank you that you gave your Holy Spirit to me without measure–I choose now to live in that fullness, and leave all the loose ends, perplexing situations and misunderstandings to you.

Instead, I live in mystical union with the Godhead.

In the name of the Father, Son and Holy Spirit!

ABOUT THE AUTHOR

David Hewitt was born in the English Midlands and grew up in the small market town of Warwick. At the age of 18 he came to Scotland to study architecture at the University of Edinburgh.

He met Maggie while spending a year working in Tanzania; they married after returning to Edinburgh and had two children. While still employed as an architect, David became increasingly involved in church leadership, and became part of a team leading Community Church Edinburgh in 2001.

In 2006, he and his wife took the unexpected (some thought 'crazy') step of selling their house to buy a redundant Victorian church on the edge of the city, which had been in use as a piano warehouse, sensing God say that 'he had an adventure' for them. They renovated the building and established Wellsprings Community as an informal, creative, grace-orientated expression of the *ecclesia,* exploring the Trinitarian faith.

David published *Reconstructing Ecclesia* (available on Amazon Kindle and in paperback, 2023) and regularly takes part in conferences or podcasts. As well as writing, he loves sailing, painting, history and nature.

Wellsprings Community regularly host workshops and events: contact **info@wellsprings.uk.net** for information or visit the website **www.wellsprings.uk.net**.

Printed in Great Britain
by Amazon

1db23482-20ef-43b3-9b8a-11fcb395ec16R01